D1083196

# ACROSS THE CREEK

# ACROSS
# THE CREEK

Faulkner Family Stories

*Jim Faulkner*

University Press of Mississippi
Jackson and London

MIDDLEBURY COLLEGE LIBRARY

ABB-0748

PS
3511
.A86
Z7828
1986

Copyright © 1986 by the University Press of Mississippi
All rights reserved
Manufactured in the United States of America

Second Printing 1987

**Library of Congress Cataloging-in Publication Data**

Faulkner, Jim, 1923-
Across the creek.

1. Faulkner, William, 1897-1962—Biography—Family.
2. Faulkner, John 1901-1963. 3. Faulkner family.
4. Novelists, American—20th century—Biography.
5. Oxford (Miss.)—Biography. 6. Oxford (Miss.)—
Social life and customs. 7. Oxford (Miss.)—Fiction.
I. Title.
PS3511.A86Z7828 1986     813'.52 [B]     86-5629
ISBN 0-87805-302-6

To the memory of
my wife Nan,
my father and mother
John and Dolly,
and my uncle William,
WHOSE SPIRITS FLOW
THROUGH THESE PAGES

# Contents

# Foreword

A writer of personality, family, and character who spends most of his years and days in his community comes to know the people, and they come to know the stories about the writer almost as well as he knows his place. William Faulkner and Oxford, Lafayette County, Mississippi, knew each other well. The county and Faulkner's fictional county, Yoknapatawpha, are not the same place, but the similarities are so great that the distinctions have never become precisely clear, and they never will.

Faulkner and his books have been discussed critically and biographically about as much as any other twentieth-century author. But it is difficult for the outside reader to understand the daily Faulkner in his hometown. A few literary people lived in Oxford, but Faulkner went out of his way as much to avoid them as he did to mingle with them. Much of his time he spent with plain people of diverse interests and a wide range of social class and wealth, but most of them were not the kind of people to become a significant part of the daily news or of history.

Many there be who have tried to describe William Faulkner, the citizen of Oxford: a number of fellow citizens of various times during Faulkner's life in Oxford have written a collection of memories; a fellow hunter has written about

Faulkner with his hunting companions and about the people who were part of the background in the stories; his two brothers who survived him have published books about him and his family; and a number of short and fugitive pieces have appeared in one form and another.

William Faulkner, the daily man of Oxford, nevertheless, is still in many details unknown to those who write about him. It is a deplorable gap in knowledge, because Faulkner was a small-town southern citizen as well as a writer of fiction, a member of small literary groups, a writer of motion picture scripts, a winner of the Nobel Prize, and a world celebrity.

Now one of Faulkner's nephews adds to the common lore about him and his community. Jimmy Faulkner is a son of William's brother John, himself the author of seven books, notably *Men Working* (about the WPA), *Dollar Cotton*, and *My Brother Bill*. Jimmy Faulkner played with a group of children who were encouraged and supervised in their youthful Faulknerian venturesomeness by John Faulkner and William Faulkner and others in the family. Jimmy Faulkner and his Uncle William ("Brother Will," Jimmy calls him) have sat together in silence, talked a little, hunted together, and lived together in a small town. Jimmy was the last Faulkner to see the great author alive. Jimmy knows the characters and the lives of the Faulkner men, their families, and their old retainers better than any Faulkner alive knows them. These stories, therefore, are appropriate and significant tales about the place and time of the leading writer of Oxford.

Jimmy knows many of the people and the episodes that William and John knew, but he tells different things about them, often in different ways. He knows the aristocrats of the county, the hunters, the farmers, the neighbors and friends, and some others. The humor, the tall tales, the adventures and misadventures of his stories have a background similar to Faulkner's own—even when there may be little close resemblance between these stories and the characters created by the brothers John and William Faulkner. Jimmy Faulkner's stories are old-fashioned in their own way. They are typical and excellent folklore, humor, history, fictionalized history, and accounts of southern life. They do, as the scholar says, shed new light on the Faulkners in episodes not known before, but they would be fun in themselves even if they did not provide new historical and literary information about the Faulkner people and country at all.

FLOYD C. WATKINS

# Preface

All resemblances in this book to the places and people of Oxford, Lafayette County, Mississippi, during my childhood are entirely intentional. With a little less than the usual embroidery of southern storytellers, these recollections are as true as I could make them.

I think I should mention, however, that two of the pieces—I have placed them last in the collection—are not actually recollections but rather stories in which fact sits side by side with fiction. "Grandfather" in the first of these, "Aunt Tee and Her Two Monuments," is John Wesley Thompson Falkner, my great-grandfather. But he died the year before I was born and therefore could not have told me the story of the two Confederate monuments as I have him doing. Readers who are familiar with the Falkner-Faulkner genealogy will no doubt discover that "Grandfather" in the second of these stories, "Grandfather Crossing the Creek," combines elements of both John Wesley Thompson Falkner and his father, Colonel William C. Falkner, my great-great-grandfather. The son is of course the Falkner who "lived in town in the big white house on South Street" that he had built so he could be close to his bank and his law office. It was the father who fought in the war. The Old Colonel was shot to death— mortally wounded—on the town square of Ripley, Mississippi, in 1889 by a former business partner. He was in his sixties then. The character in my story lives into his nineties and simply dies at home in bed.

The stories in this book were written over a period of several years, and some of them originally appeared in the *Southern Review, Delta Review, Mississippi Review,* and *Delta Heritage*, though in a somewhat different form. I would like to acknowledge publication by those magazines. I thank Jo Marshall of Jefferson State Junior College, Birmingham, for convincing me that I needed to record these stories and for working with me as I did so. I would especially like to express my deep appreciation to Floyd C. Watkins of Emory University, whose untiring efforts and encouragement caused this collection to happen.

JIM FAULKNER

# ACROSS THE CREEK

# Roasting Black Buster

PRESIDENT ROOSEVELT was well into his second term in the White House, and the country was creeping out of the Big Depression, not as fast as some of our leaders would like us to believe, but it was. There were WPA projects and other government programs that gave people jobs, and you'd see tenant farmers riding to town in homemade buses and then riding back that afternoon after quitting time, back to their little hillside farms. The CCC camps around the North Mississippi hills were giving boys and men barracks homes like they would know later when they were mobilized in the army during World War II, and mess halls too, like the army, and fifteen dollars in exchange for a month's work planting seedling pine trees to stop the erosion on the worn-out farms that they had helped to cause by laziness and neglect. It was more money than any of them had ever seen at one time in their lives except maybe in a crap game or at a moonshine still.

It was during these years that my father, John, and his brother William—I called him Brother Will—decided to buy a farm in Lafayette County, where they were raised and

3

where they had hunted as boys and young men before they were married. They had been closer then, but had gone their separate ways to make their places in the world, or at least in Mississippi. Now they were coming back together with the farm as a common interest. They found "The Farm," as we called it, but which Brother Will at times called Greenfield, on Puskus Creek in the northeast part of the county. They raised cattle and especially mules—probably because Brother Will liked mules and felt sorry for them because each one was his own self, neither horse nor jack, and unable to leave sons or daughters to propagate his own breed. We raised them to sell at a time when farmers were beginning to buy tractors that they wouldn't need to feed through the winter. Brother Will wanted mules, so we raised mules.

Early in the spring we moved out to the farm to get ready for the cattle and for the jack—named Big Shot—and the mares to raise mule colts. The row crops that we grew on the farm were to feed the cows and horses and mules—like corn and hay and peas. The families who moved there with us planted their own gardens, but we planted a big one to be sure that everybody on the place would have enough to last all summer long and still have enough to can and preserve to go through the winter, too. My mother, Dolly, took charge of this. She asked for and got one of the men (named Lightning—not because of his speed, but the lack of it) who lived on the place to help make the garden produce enough for all of us. Rains that spring were scarce and the gardens and the cornfields and hayfields were dry. June came on hot and dry, not with the blue skies of late spring and early summer, but with hazy hot skies that dried out the ground and made the early corn leaves creak and rustle when they swayed in the soft hot breezes that came through the fields.

On a morning early in June, Dolly had Lightning working in the garden against his wishes. He was born and raised in the country, and he figured that since this was our first year to live outside of town he knew more about it than Dolly did. He always let her know that he either doubted her or disagreed with her. This particular morning Dolly was about five rows away from Lightning, who was sticking cane poles in the ground for the bean vines to run on. He turned around to pick up another bean pole, and a long black snake crawled by just a few rows away.

Lightning yelled, "SNAKE!" and jumped the five rows and landed beside Dolly. His eyes were big and excited, and he was breathing hard. He pointed back at the snake and said, "See 'at un? He's a big un, ain't he?"

Calm as always, Dolly said, "Lightning, go kill that snake and hang him belly-up on the fence and we will get a rain in three days. We need it real bad for the gardens and fields. They are drying up."

"Yassum." Lightning looked at Dolly like he wondered what these town folks who had just moved out here in the country would try to tell him when he had been farming and gardening all his life. He took his hoe and reached as far out as the handle would let him, and with a good hard downward chop that almost broke the handle he cut the snake's head off.

Dolly, watching from across the rows, said, "Now, take him to that fence over there and hang him belly-side up, and we'll get that rain, if what the old folks say is right."

Lightning did as he was told, cutting his eyes skeptically at Dolly. He took the long black shiny body in the crook of the blade of the hoe with the tail dragging, walked across the rows of the garden, and laid the snake belly-side up across the top strand of the fence. Its head, or what was left of that end

5

of it, almost touched the ground on one side, and the tail did touch on the other side.

Lightning backed up and looked at the snake, still moving from muscle spasms, flinching every time it moved, and said, "He sho wuz a big un—musta been da granddaddy uv 'em all." Holding his hoe midway down the handle with the blade forward and down, he crossed the rows back to where Dolly was standing and asked, "Missus, is 'at right 'bout 'at rain you sayed 'ud come in lessen three days ifen you hung a snake belly-side up crost a fence?"

Dolly nodded and said, "That's what I've always heard. Hang him belly-side up across a fence and it'll rain in three days every time. Now let's get back to sticking these poles in the ground so the beans will have something to run on when they grow, and we'll have some food to eat this winter."

The rest of the day the sun bore down from a hot hazy pale blue cloudless sky, and Lightning looked up every few minutes at the glaring sun, then at Dolly, and then at the snake. The next day and the next one, too, the sun bore down again on Dolly and Lightning—still without a cloud in the sky and no sign of rain. The third morning broke hazy clear and still promised another hot day. Dolly and Lightning were back in the garden early. The snake on the fence was getting rank, and Lightning grew more doubtful as the hours went by.

Dinner time came, and Dolly said, "Lightning, let's go to dinner and get back here as soon this afternoon as we can and we'll get through early."

"Yassum, hit's gettin' on tow'ds da end uv 'at third day now, an' 'at ole black snake ain't done nuthin' yet but stink."

Dolly had forgotten that she had told Lightning about the snake hanging belly-up on the fence and causing a rain in three

6

days, so she said, "Go on and get something to eat and we'll worry about that later."

Lightning had just walked inside his house for dinner and Dolly into hers when a loud clap of thunder rolled over and through the farm and a cloud began building in the west. Lightning ran to his front porch and watched the sky grow darker and the rolling black storm clouds moving toward him in front of the high towering boiling thundercloud. The wind roared like a locomotive; the leaves rustled; then the limbs bent and the tree trunks leaned away, giving with the wind.

Lightning yelled, "Shet da dohs—she's a comin'."

The rain came first in big scattered drops, then increased to waving sheets of water. Lightning watched through a small crack that he had left in the door till the cold clear driving rain ran him back and made him close it. The wind kept blowing and rocking his house and rattling the windows and shaking everything not tied down. Lightning ran from the front door to the back, latching what he could; then he yelled to Jody May, his wife, "Come on an' git un'er da bed; dis hyar's gonna be a bad un."

The storm moved on to the east, leaving branches and leaves torn from the trees scattered around the yard and water in puddles and running down the furrows in the gardens and fields, giving new life to the plants in the dried-out ground. Lightning peeped out his door when the wind calmed down and the rain slowed from a downpour to a few scattered drops and then to drops falling from the clean green leaves and shrubs and dripping off the edges of the roof. He ran to the Big House, stepping around puddles and heavy wet grass and the mud in the path. He banged on the back door, not taking time to ring the bell hanging next to the steps. Dolly

7

opened the door and looked at him standing big-eyed and stuttering, believing now in Dolly's prophecy. "Missus, don't you recon' 'at snake what we hung belly-up on 'at fence wuz too big an' hit brang us too much rain an' win' all at onct?"

"Lightning, the next time we need a rain we'll just hang a small one up there, so we'll just get a good shower."

"Yassum, 'at un wuz jus' too much at onct."

Well, the storm with all the rain helped the garden and the crops. It brought back the pastures and made the corn turn from a light greenish yellow to a healthy dark green, and the vegetable garden took on new life. A few days later, about the middle of June, John and Brother Will were standing by the barn looking across the fence at James plowing a pair of mules that were pulling a middle buster down a furrow with the wings of the plow sweeping dirt up on the young cornstalks on either side that were high enough to touch the knees of the mules. In a few days they would be so tall that the double tree attached to the plow would break them down. My father and my uncle decided then that the crops would be good that year and that they would have a Fourth of July picnic and invite all the neighbors and friends from town out to see the farm and what they had done with it.

Uncle Ned lived in one of the houses on the farm, and since he had been with the family for five generations he occupied a position of authority and respect and was the envy of the other people on the place. All he really had to do was milk our two cows twice a day, sit under the big oak trees by the pond in the pasture, and tell us stories about the old days during the Big War and about the people in our family who had been here before us. He knew all about them, and the animals, too, including the livestock that we had now. He even named them.

One day a shoat ran past him while he was walking down the hill from the house to the barn slowly swinging the milk bucket to the rhythm of his shuffling gait. Uncle Ned stopped and turned and looked at him for a minute and said, "Well, Suh. Ah knows jus' who you is. You looks jus' lak yo' pappy." He did, too, because we just had one boar hog on the farm.

He named every male animal on the place "Black Buster" if he had at least one black hair somewhere on him. Our small herd of cows needed upgrading for beef cattle, so Brother Will bought a young herd bull—a registered Black Angus yearling that was fat and shiny and the envy of the farmers in the neighborhood. Just as soon as he walked across the pasture, Uncle Ned said, "Yassuh, he's sho nuff a fine un, a real buster."

So right then he was Black Buster. We already had one bull calf named Black Buster. He was out of one of the Jersey milk cows that Uncle Ned milked every day. To "freshen" her we had turned her in with a black bull that was not nearly as fine a bull as our registered Black Buster, and she had brought this small black bull calf that Uncle Ned had said while he was milking Black Jersey, his mother, "Git back, you little buster; Ah'll leave you plenty uv dinna." And he became another Black Buster.

That June when John and Brother Will decided to have the Fourth of July barbecue Brother Will came out from town every few days to help with the plans and to check on things. The early corn would be in the roasting-ear stage at just the right time. Brother Will knew that Uncle Jim, a man who lived up the road from the farm, had just made two gallons of corn whiskey that we could have, but we would have to send for it. Uncle Jim wouldn't bring it for fear of being caught by the sheriff. Brother Will figured that Chooky, my eleven-year-old brother, was the only one young enough not to have tasted whiskey yet, so he was the one to be trusted with that much corn whiskey all at one time to get back with the same amount that he left with from Uncle Jim's house. So Chooky was to take two croker sacks and a horse and leave early in the morning to get the whiskey so the cooks and any visitors who came the day before could enjoy a night around the fire telling stories and tasting the cooking meat and the recent corn drippings from Uncle Jim's still.

John and Brother Will thought that we should have fried catfish, too, so we loaded the wagon with camping gear and food enough for a couple of days, and with James and Renzi driving a pair of mules, Tom and Jeff, we set out for a place we knew in the river bottom where Puskus Creek and Cypress Creek run into the Tallahatchie River. We could catch enough catfish in two days and nights for everybody. It was about half a day's trip down the hot dusty road with our two black and tan hounds, Nip and Tuck, trotting along under the wagon in the shade and in front of the little dust plumes following the iron-rim wheels.

We made camp on the creek bank about an hour before first dark with the wagon in the center and the mules in a small rope corral with a bale of hay and a few ears of corn to keep them satisfied. We had bait for the fishhooks along with the hooks and string and lead sinkers in the wagon. James and I cut poles along the creek bank, and for about two hundred yards on either side stuck them in the soft mud just above water level so that the line with the hook and bait would be about five feet out in the creek and about a foot below the surface of the gently flowing current where the catfish fed off the berries and bugs that came within reach.

After James and I checked the hooks all night, hoping to

catch a hundred or so fish that weren't there, and fought hungry mosquitoes that attacked us like they hadn't had a decent meal all summer, we had breakfast about sunrise and decided that the barbecue would have to do without the five small blue channel catfish that we just happened to snag on our baited hooks. After breakfast two tired sleepy fishermen harnessed and backed two rested mules into the traces of the wagon, and we retraced the steps of the mules' sharp dainty hoofprints the four dusty miles back to Greenfield. The mules—not tired after resting all night, but just as flop-eared as if they were—plodded in their tireless walk, switching their tails at an occasional horsefly. Nip and Tuck, acting like the two lazy hounds that they were, trotted underneath the wagon in the only shade that moved in time with the mules' pace.

John was disgusted because we hadn't caught enough fish even to talk about, Renzi and Chooky were contented just to be moving and alive on a good hot summer day, Dolly wasn't happy about any part of it, and James and I were worn out from fishing all night. More to himself than anybody else, John said, "I guess this will have to be more of a beef barbecue than fish or anything, except folks' brains that might be cooked from corn whiskey and what they might bring with them, and that won't be much because they'll expect us to furnish it all no matter what."

The road back to Greenfield was hotter and dustier than it had been going the other way the day before. Every time we passed a house people waved and spoke and their dogs came running out to bark at Nip and Tuck until we were past what they considered their territory; then they would go back and flop down in the shade under their porch or a tree. Uncle Ned heard the iron tires on the wagon wheels popping and grinding on what little gravel we had on the road and the trace chains rattling and clanking as we came down the hill to the front gate. He met us there and held it open while we drove through, then followed us to the barn to unharness Tom and Jeff and put the wagon under the shed next to the corn crib. When the wagon was unloaded and everything put up, Uncle Ned, knowing already and probably even before we left that there would be no fish to speak of, said to John, "Mist' John, yestiddy Mist' Bill, he wuz out hyar a'ter y'all lef' an' he sayed to dress out Black Buster an' we'd barbecue him fo' a Fo'th uv July picnic."

John stopped what he was doing and looked at Uncle Ned and said, "Now, Uncle Ned, Bill didn't say that. That's the new full-blooded 'paper' bull he got for our cows. He wouldn't want us to cook him." Then John thought a minute and said, "Well, Bill is curious sometimes and this is just the sort of thing he'd do. He would want the best for his company."

"Yassuh, he sho sayed it, an' ifen we's gonna have anythin' to cook fo' all 'ese folks what we's got comin' out chere we better git at it, 'cause jus' two days from now da Fo'th's gonna be hyar."

"Well, all right, go get some of the men and get him ready. We'd better start cooking tomorrow night to be ready the next day. Have somebody dig a pit and cut some hickory and get a good fire going so the coals will be good for cooking all night, tomorrow night. Then have somebody go to the cornfield and get some roasting ears. Be sure that they get plenty, we don't want to run out. Then tomorrow we'll send Chooky up to Uncle Jim's after that two gallons of whiskey."

"Yassuh, I'll git 'em started rat now, diggin' an' bringin' in some hick'ry sticks an' logs."

Uncle Ned ambled off with an air of authority and began

to direct everything like he always did, but John's having told him to do it this time made him even more bossy. The last thing I heard before I dropped off to sleep on our sleeping porch that afternoon, tired from no sleep after fishing the night before, was Uncle Ned down in the pasture by the pond under the big oak trees telling two or three men exactly how to dig the pit and build the fire to cook Black Buster.

The next morning before the sun came over the hill behind Uncle Oscar's house we were all down around the picnic ground where the activity was. Even Uncle Oscar was already there. He couldn't stand anything going on without being there himself. He had a house full of children. Some were his and his wife Maggie's and some were kinfolks' children that had come to live with them. This morning he had told Maggie he had to step over to the commissary to get a few things for breakfast, but what he really wanted to do was hang around us and watch what was happening.

We knew when Uncle Oscar was overdue back home because we could hear Maggie calling him all the way to our house. Her voice would carry over the two hills between us, even against the wind. He was leaning against a tree relaxed and watching, probably had forgotten, too, that he had told Maggie he wouldn't be gone long, when he heard her call, and he jumped. We heard Maggie's voice, too, high and strong coming over the hill.

She yelled, "Oscar—uh—Oscar."

He answered like he always did, "Whooo—eeee."

She yelled again, "Come back by the tater patch an' bring some to the house fo' dinna."

Uncle Oscar snatched his old torn sweaty straw hat off his head and slapped it against his faded patched blue overall-covered leg and said, "Hot damn, her an' all 'em chilluns gonna have 'em all et up fo' Ah can git 'em all dug up." He trudged on over the hill toward the potato patch and home, but we knew we'd see him again before the sun got much higher. He just couldn't stay away. And we were right, he was back before the sun was straight up overhead, and he even helped some, too, now. Things were picking up. The beef, all four hundred pounds of it, was cleaned and cut up ready for the fire that was blazing now and later would simmer down to the red hot hickory coals that would cook the meat all night so it would be ready for the early arrivals the next morning and the cooks and workers even earlier. James and Renzi brought in croker sacks full of green corn to roast in the hot coals, and Chooky did make it to Uncle Jim's house and back with two jugs of whiskey tied in the croker sacks so that one was hanging on either side of the horse in the saddle in front of him.

Brother Will didn't get to the farm that day at all. But he did get there early the next morning so he would be there when the first ones came out from town on the day of the Fourth of July picnic. We had been up since before daylight, and some of the men hadn't even been to bed, just slept a few minutes now and then when they could, while the meat and roasting ears were simmering and roasting in the pit of red hot coals. John was standing on one side of the pit telling Mac how to cook and when to turn the meat and watching James and Renzi rolling up logs and anything else to use for seats and tables, with a tin cup in his hand, sipping and tasting some of Uncle Jim's latest run that Chooky had brought back the day before, when Brother Will drove up to the gate. Uncle Ned could always tell when it was time for him to come in, and he would manage to get to the gate to have it open, so he would know that he, Uncle Ned, was there thinking about him.

Brother Will drove up to his favorite parking place under the persimmon trees next to the commissary just up the hill from where we were cooking Black Buster. He got out of his old open touring car with the ragged top that we had to wear raincoats in when it rained, and in his slow easy deliberate way walked in that reared-back manner of his back down the hill to the picnic ground. He sat down on one of the long logs and Uncle Ned already had a tin cup about half full of Uncle Jim's Special waiting for him.

We could look across Puskus Creek bottom toward the gravel road that everybody called the Rock. It was the main road to town and the only gravel road in our part of the country, and we could see the plumes of dust following the wagons and cars coming to the barbecue. Looking at the wagons and cars making their way to Greenfield, John said to James that it looked like our farm wouldn't be big enough to hold all the people and he was worried that we might run out of food and drink. The day was clear and hot, and the cornfields and hayfields were lush and green after the snake's thunderstorm.

Brother Will accepted the cup from Uncle Ned, saying, "Many thanks, this ought to go good, if Uncle Jim made it like he always does." Then he got up from his log and spoke to some of the early comers as he passed them on the way to where John was standing by the barbecue pit watching Mac turn the meat. He stood a few minutes just looking and breathing in the sweet tantalizing aroma of cooking beef. Then he said to John, "That sho is gonna be some good eatin'."

John said, "By golly, it ought to be." He was thinking about that full-blooded Black Angus bull that they were cooking.

About that time Brother Will lifted the cup to his lips and, raising his eyes as he tilted his head back, still with the cup to his lips so a small sip of Uncle Jim's Special would trickle into his mouth and down his throat, looked across the pasture and saw the little black Jersey bull. Then he looked down at the cooking meat, and back at the bull again in disbelief. He came to life and pointed down at the pit and almost shouted, "Who is that?"

John said, "That's Black Buster."

Brother Will, with his arm extended all the way pointing at the Jersey bull on the hill, said, "That's Black Buster!"

John said again, pointing at the cooking meat, "That's Black Buster."

Brother Will, knowing then what had happened, said, "Damn Uncle Ned for naming everything on the place Black Buster." He walked back to the log and sat down, looking dejected and undone, his arms resting on his knees and one hand hanging lax between his legs, the other holding the tin cup, and his head down shaking slowly from side to side. Then he raised his head, put the cup to his mouth, and drained it all in one gulp, set the cup down on the log next to him, looked at the fire, still shaking his head, and said, "He was my prize bull. I just can't eat him."

Everybody else did though, and the meat "sho was good eatin'," just like he said it was going to be.

John, always the optimist, made up this rhyme about it:

> E Pluribus Unum
> In God We Trust
> If you see Brother Will
> Don't mention Black Bust.

# The Picture
# of John and Brother Will

I N JULY OF 1949 Phil Mullen, the editor of the weekly
newspaper in Oxford, took a picture of John and Brother
Will standing together in our front yard. It was the first
picture to be taken of just the two Faulkner boys since a
traveling photographer came through town and posed them
on their ponies in front of Big Dad and Nannie's house on
Second South Street and later in the parlor after Nannie and
Granny scrubbed them till their faces shone like polished red
apples. The main reason Brother Will was in our front yard
was that the grass had grown too tall and John had fixed my
brand new power lawnmower so that it wouldn't work. The
other reason was that I had just met Nan Watson from
Rimrock, Arizona, a stewardess for American Airlines
stationed in Memphis. I had known her for about a month
and had driven to Memphis to see her so much that Guy
Rogers accused me of being mad at the highway department
and trying to wear out the road from Oxford to Memphis.

Oxford is a small town and everybody not only knows
everybody else, they know their goings on as well. Back in
that summer of 1949 all of my family—Nannie (my grand-

mother) and John and Dolly (my father and mother) and aunts and uncles and cousins and even Uncle Ned—were curious about my new interest in Memphis. Uncle Ned wasn't just curious; he was a little worried, too, because he felt like he owned all of us and was responsible to my great-great-grandfather, Colonel William C. Falkner, the "Old Colonel," who was really the beginning of our family, and long since gone. Uncle Ned was born a slave on the Old Colonel's place and would never leave after the Big War. He said that he had never been freed, so he stayed with the family and owned us, and the longer he lived the more of us he collected.

The time had come when it seemed like the only thing for me to do was to bring Nan to Oxford to meet the family and give all the folks in town a chance to see her. But there was one problem: the front yard. A man just couldn't bring a girl home for the first time with the yard so grown-up and shaggy that a flock of preening peacocks could get lost in it.

The front yard at our house covered more than an acre; counting the east side yard where the flower garden used to be and the back yard, too, there are nearly two acres, and it seems about twice that big when you're halfway through mowing it on a hot summer day. I had cut those two acres every Friday and Saturday from the time I was big enough to push a lawnmower until I moved into my own house (except for the four years during World War II). And what I used was a regular pushing mower, not one of those with a motor attached to it to make it move along by itself. I think I might even have wanted the war to last a little longer, because I knew that lawnmower would be waiting for me when I got back. I had pushed and sweated and cussed grass until I declared that one day I would have a power mower if I had to keep on cutting that big yard every week in the summertime as long as I lived in John's house (and there was no other place I wanted to be).

It was in the third summer after I had gotten back home from the war and about two weeks before Nan was to come to Oxford that the old pushing-type mower just quit. I was glad that it wore out before I did, because I felt as if I had finally beaten one of my enemies that wouldn't let me grow up. That mower had robbed me of many Friday afternoons and Saturdays. I had pushed it up and down the yard so many times that I felt like a bird dog on a wire run. Whenever I fought that mower, there was a shower of grass blowing out the back; most of it ended up in my shoes and the cuffs of my pants, and when I went in the house, it all fell out on the floor, and Dolly didn't like that. I wouldn't cut the grass barefooted because I'd been told that a man couldn't balance well with a big toe gone.

Nan was coming to Oxford, and it was time to get a new lawnmower because the old one was worn out and the grass in our front yard had grown past the joking stage. The power lawnmower that I bought must have been the first and only machine that this particular company ever made. Maybe a group of mad mechanics had made it as a joke on American lawnmower pushers. But I had to have one right then, and this was the only power mower I could find in Oxford. Anyway, it looked better to me than that worn-out weekend-spoiler that I had been using.

My father, John, could do anything with his hands. He could take a pair of pliers and a screwdriver and a coat hanger and make the world stop and turn backwards if he set his mind to it. The morning I brought the new power lawnmower home John was sitting in his summertime place, a swing under

19

a maple tree in the front yard, with the grass up above his ankles. He watched me as I unloaded it from the back of the car and rolled it in front of the swing for him to see. He looked it over real good, then said, "Well, sir, look what you've got. Let's crank it up and see what she'll do."

I wound the starter rope around the pulley and gave it a good healthy pull. Nothing—not even a sputter. That shiny hunk of mismatched metal just sat there like a stubborn mule. Three, maybe four more pulls, and still nothing. The motor was supposed to be doing the work, not I. If there was ever anything made to harass mankind, it must have been a gasoline engine that has to be started with a rope. A hand-cranked motor has caused more cussing and more drinking and more men to stomp out the back door than all the jackleg whiskey makers in the red clay hills of north Mississippi.

Well, finally the infernal machine did start and even ran for a little while. I thought that since I had gone to all the trouble to get it started, I should at least cut part of the yard before I turned it off. I made two trips back and forth in front of John, and then I saw him waving me to come back to where he was watching from the swing. I ran the mower right up to his feet, just like he told me to, and turned the motor off, and that was the last time it ran even halfway right until we gave it away.

John said, "Now I know how come it wouldn't start. And I can make it run better, too. Run in the house and get my pliers and screwdriver so I can fix it. The governor needs to be loosened up so it won't choke down in that tall grass."

I tried to explain to him that if he worked on it at all the warranty wouldn't be any good, but he said the warranty wasn't any good anyhow, and besides, he was an engineer and knew more about the mower than the people who made it. I didn't doubt that he was right, but it was *my* new mower and I didn't want it messed up the first day. However, I never did win an argument from him, and he was my father, so I got the pliers and the screwdriver. I guess my mistake was not getting a coat hanger, too.

Before the day was over we tore the engine down, broke the governor, and fixed the motor so it would run the mower as long as I stayed in short grass and used one hand to guide it, which meant that I had to walk stooped over like a bear with the other hand on the gas feed to hold it open. I saw right quick that at the rate I was going I couldn't get the grass cut in the two weeks left before Nan came. I looked around from my bear-walking-hand-on-gas-feed position and saw John back sitting in the swing watching the cars go by, completely disinterested in what he had done to my new mower and to me. I managed to get that sputtering machine back to where he was sitting and asked him what we were going to do now. He said, "Take it back."

I said, "We can't."

He said, "Let's eat supper."

For the next few days, while the grass grew taller and taller, I left the mower parked in front of the swing so John would have to see it if he sat in his usual place and watched the cars go by. He sat in the swing all right, all day every day, but he ignored my mower. And he wouldn't talk about it at breakfast or dinner or supper. Finally, a couple of days before Nan was due, I told John that he had to think of something. That was a mistake. He said, "Bill has just bought himself a new David Bradley garden tractor with a mowing blade on it. How about going down to his house and getting him to lend it to you?"

Brother Will never said no to me in his life, although there were times when I'm sure he wanted to and other times when he should have and didn't. John knew Brother Will would let me have that tractor and that was the reason he sent me. I didn't want to go down to Brother Will's house and ask him for his new tractor, but it looked like the only way to get that big yard cut in time, so I went.

Brother Will's house was about five hundred yards from ours through Brown's pasture and a small patch of woods, but it was a good mile around by University Avenue, then to the end of Second South Street, and a short way down the Old Taylor Road to the front gate and his "Private Keep Out" sign. When I got to Brother Will's house, he was in the backyard admiring his new red garden tractor. It already had one dent in it, where he had run it up on the back porch and hit the house, hanging onto the handles yelling "Whoa!" He had cranked it in gear with the gas full on before he had read the manual telling him how to stop it.

We talked about his new David Bradley, and we both agreed that it was a good buy and that every man should own one just exactly like it. It took a bit to work up to a good opening in the conversation, because you just don't haul off and ask a man to let you use his brand new play-pretty when it is as new as that tractor was, without picking just the right time to do it. Well, I did. I told him that I had a problem and that John had sent me down to borrow his new David Bradley with the mowing attachment. He didn't really look at me in disbelief, but it took a long time for him to answer. He finally said, "Well, all right, Jim. But please be careful and bring it back."

He gave me a long lecture on what to do and what not to do with the tractor. I felt bad about taking it and running the risk of something happening to it, but I needed a mowing machine, so I took it. I ran it out in the street all the way home because the street was smoother than the walk. I couldn't let anything happen to Brother Will's David Bradley while I had it.

I did get the grass cut in time, and I parked Brother Will's tractor beside my power lawnmower in front of the swing so John could see it. I figured that since I had gotten it from Brother Will and done all the work, he could take it back or at least go with me while I did, but he didn't even suggest it. He had already completely dismissed that lawnmower from his mind, and there the two mowing machines stayed all the time Nan was in Oxford, with John just sitting in his swing looking over them at the cars going by.

Just a few days after Nan had gone back to Memphis after that first visit I was sitting in the swing with John, foolishly wondering just which one of us would take the David Bradley back, when I saw Brother Will and his hired boy, Broadus, coming up the front walk toward us. I could tell by the way he walked and looked at the ground that he wasn't happy at all. I wished that I could have been someplace else right then, but there didn't seem to be any way, so I just sat there and waited.

Brother Will stopped in front of us, with Broadus standing a few paces behind him. He looked at his tractor, then at me, then at John, and said, "John, you haven't brought my tractor home yet."

John could always think faster than Brother Will; that's one reason they were so funny when they were together. He looked up from his seat in the swing with his blue eyes twinkling and grinned and said, "Naw, Bill, but least I didn't loan it to somebody else."

That didn't set well at all with Brother Will, considering the frame of mind he was in about that pet tractor of his. I could usually tell what his mood was by the way he turned a penny matchbox between his thumb and trigger finger, and he was turning it a little faster than normal. I kept a straight face until I just couldn't hold it any longer and had to laugh. He did grin, then, but he didn't laugh. In fact, I don't think Brother Will knew how to laugh. When he got tickled, all he could do was chuckle. I could tell when he was supposed to be laughing by watching his eyes. They would crinkle at the corners and sparkle. His eyes told more about his moods than anything else about him. When he was mad they would turn to a flashing black, but during his happy times they were a soft brown. They were that soft brown this time, because I really think he was relieved that John hadn't loaned it to somebody else.

Brother Will turned to the tractor, dismissing us and everything else from his mind, but showing Broadus how to start the David Bradley and take care of it on the way home. John and Brother Will were just alike that way: they could ignore something to the point where anything that happened to be going on around them didn't even exist. While Broadus was getting the lecture on the tractor, I heard a car pull up in the driveway behind us. Phil Mullen had just happened to drive by and he saw John and Brother Will together. He got out of his car with a camera in his hand and said, "Y'all stand right there."

Brother Will stepped back behind the swing when Phil aimed the camera. Phil said, "Come on now, Bill, you and John stand out here in the sun so I can get this picture."

Brother Will told Phil that he had supposed he wanted a picture of his new David Bradley tractor. His eyes were soft and twinkling now, and so were John's. Phil said, "Damn that tractor! Give me a picture of a mule any day!"

He said it was the only time he had ever seen the two of

them together when he had a camera and as a friend and editor of their hometown newspaper he felt that he couldn't miss this opportunity. Both John and Brother Will respected Phil Mullen a great deal, and he in turn respected them and their desire for privacy, so they moved away from the mower and tractor and stood together in the sunshine for Phil to shoot the picture.

As Phil was leaving, he thanked John and Brother Will and said the picture would be famous someday and it would make him well known for taking it. John said, "I sure hope it does for you, Phil."

The grass looks pretty good in the picture, and you can't see any feelings about the tractor in the eyes of either brother.

# The Battle in Bailey's Woods

W E PLAYED HARD in Oxford when we were growing up back in the 1930s, not with store-bought toys but with things that we made ourselves after getting ideas from the Saturday morning picture shows that always had Westerns with our favorite cowboys, like Tom Mix and Hoot Gibson and Ken Maynard, riding across the prairie chasing and shooting the bad guys and Indians. We didn't really have good and bad guys in Oxford. The town wasn't that big and we weren't worldly wise enough to be bad, so we would choose up sides or identify ourselves by the name of the street that we lived on: the Second South Street Boys, the South Street Boys, the University Avenue Boys, the Lake Street Boys. About the most we could muster on any street would be from five to eight boys close to the same age. At times when we were short of boys because of mumps or chicken pox (or because some of our mothers made us stay at home and help around the house or yard) we had to mix together the boys from different streets so we could have enough to choose sides and have a good cowboy and Indian rubber gun war.

This kind of warfare began when we found out that the service stations were throwing away old innertubes that could no longer be patched and used again and that they would give them to us just to get rid of them. We cut rubber bands that would shoot ten yards or more when stretched a little and suddenly released or that would sling a rock a good fifty yards when pulled way back. The best rubber came from truck tire innertubes, which were thicker and a lot stronger than the ones that came from regular passenger car tires. From boards we cut out crudely shaped pistols about a foot and a half long. We would stretch one of our rubber bands over the end of the barrel and pull the other end back to be hooked in the mouth of a clothespin attached to the handle. When we pressed down on the clothespin its mouth opened and the rubber band shot out. We could aim the gun and with a little practice hit an enemy nearly every time within the ten-yard range, even when he was running. If we tied a knot in the rubber band, it would really sting and raise a red welt on bare skin.

It took three hits to put a man out of action. The side that had the last one alive won the battle, and some real honest-to-goodness fights came from arguments about how many hits somebody had and who was dead and who was not. In Oxford each house sat on a lot large enough to have a garden and a chicken yard and a pigpen and a pasture for horses and milk cows and a barn. The barn in the back of the house was perfect for rubber gun fights.

Usually four or five boys would get in a barn loft and defend it, while another four or five would attack from the ground. Battles would last about an hour; then we would swap places after we had gathered up enough rubber bands for ammunition in a new engagement. Occasionally somebody would get hit in the eye and that would end the fighting

27

for a while until he stopped crying and his eye quit hurting. We all would have red welts on exposed skin.

John, my father, and Brother Will, my uncle, got interested in what we were doing and gave us names like "Buzzard Bill, the Bloody Butcher from Bounding Billows," "Keen Kut Kookie, the Crying Kid from Crabapple Corners," "Pistol Pete, the Plundering Pirate from Powder Point," and "Mangling Mac, the Man-Eating Maniac from Murder Mountain."

Brother Will's stable didn't have enough stalls for a good rubber gun fight, but a barn in our pasture was just right, and we used it for nearly all of our battles until one day when John came out a little early to milk our cow. He was sitting on his stool milking and the cow was about half asleep, contentedly eating. Chooky, my little brother, "Keen Kut Kookie, the Crying Kid from Crabapple Corners," thought he saw one of the enemy run into the end stall where John was milking. As Chooky ran past the door of the stall he fired two shots through the open door. One shot was a direct hit on the cow's back end. She jumped to the other side of the stall, leaving John sitting in the middle of the stall with the partially filled bucket of milk in front of him. Later he said that Chooky shot that cow right out of his hands. When the cow refused to give any more milk that afternoon, John made a rule that we couldn't have rubber gun wars in the barn while he was milking. So we wouldn't have to stop a battle just for a cow to be milked, we got together with the rest of the boys in our part of town and decided to build a clubhouse in a big pasture used by townspeople to graze their milk cows during the day.

The next day we all went to the woods that bordered the pasture and with axes and saws borrowed from tool boxes without the owner knowing it cut four gum saplings long enough to support a clubhouse about ten feet off the ground. It took the better part of a week—with time out for going to see Tom Mix and Hoot Gibson in their latest escapades and for swimming in our favorite swimming hole in the Yocona River just south of town—to build on top of the four gum posts a straw hut big enough for about six boys. We figured that if the only entrance was by means of a rope ladder that could be pulled up through the trapdoor in the floor we could defend our clubhouse against any gang likely to attack us. We had used the most available materials that were around, including limbs and small trees that still had leaves on them. We did step through the floor sometimes because the leaves would hide a space that we had left between two limbs. It was easy to part the leaves anywhere in the walls or floor and look inside and watch for the enemy. We left holes in the walls on all four sides to shoot our rubber guns through. We thought that we were invincible, and during the first two battles we were. But when we went to the picture show on Saturday morning and saw some soldiers defending their fort with a cannon against an Indian attack we decided that to make our clubhouse more of a fort and more impregnable from attack by all comers at any time we would have to have a cannon.

We rummaged around in some of our favorite playing places and found an old cast-iron sewer pipe about three feet long and four inches in diameter. It looked like it would be just right for our cannon. We mounted it on blocks in our clubhouse and cut a big opening in each side so we could shoot at the enemy no matter from which direction he attacked. The next thing we needed was ammunition for the cannon. Brother Will liked to play croquet in his front yard at Rowan Oak, just over the hill from where we were building and fortifying our clubhouse. He had just bought a new croquet set and the wooden balls were about the right size for our cannon. I knew he went to town to get his mail early each morning, so the next day while he was gone I borrowed four of his new croquet balls. The next thing was to find some powder to fire the cannon balls. Nearly all of our fathers and older brothers were hunters and kept shotgun shells all year long. Brother Will's house was the nearest. I went there again while he was making his morning trip to the post office and gathered as many shells as I could put in my pockets. We opened some of them, got a heaping cupful of black powder, and put it all in our cannon.

We charged the cannon with a mop, just like Tom Mix, ramming the powder home against the wooden plug in the back of the cast-iron pipe (cut from a sapling and driven into the back of the pipe with a big hammer). Then with old newspapers we made wadding to hold the powder in place and rammed it home with the mop. Intending to knock two of our enemy out of action with one firing, we put a couple of croquet balls in the cannon. Loaded and primed, ready to be fired in defense of our clubhouse during the next battle, it sat there, its black muzzle looking out the porthole defiantly, a friend and protector to us but formidable and threatening to our enemy.

On Saturday morning before the big battle that almost undid Oxford we saw another movie in which a cannon saved a fort from a big Indian attack. We met that afternoon right after dinner and climbed up into our clubhouse and arranged our rubber bands and guns so that they would be in easy reach when the fight began. The five of us in the clubhouse felt secure with the rope ladder pulled up and the trap door closed and enough rubber bands to last till our mothers called us in for supper. We waited for the inevitable attack from the enemy we had challenged during the picture show that morning.

Right on schedule we saw the main attack coming over a small hill—just as the enemy had warned they would—that is, as soon as their mothers would let them out of the house after dinner. The six boys were running fast. Each one had two rubber guns and a belt around a shirtless waist for carrying extra rubber bands. Although one of the attackers stepped on a sticker with his bare foot and they had to stop and pull it out before they could resume their attack, the invading force made it to within a few feet of our clubhouse before they had to retreat and reload. We fought for a while like we were inside a circle of wagons from a wagon train and Indians were attacking us. Occasionally one would dart within range and shoot a couple of times, then run back among his friends out of our range so he could stretch another rubber band on his gun. Neither side could score a hit, much less the three that it took to kill a man. The battle became a stalemate and uninteresting, and we watched through our gun openings while the enemy gathered and held a council of war. They broke up their talk and began throwing rocks at us; once in a while a rock came through the brush walls without doing any damage, but it made us keep our heads down. Then we realized that one of the enemy had been missing for some time. He came back and stopped behind a tree close to our clubhouse. We couldn't see what it was he was carrying, but it seemed important to the attackers.

Again the rocks started coming, this time so fast that we had to stay back from the brush walls to keep from being hit by the ones that penetrated our clubhouse walls. When the barrage let up, we looked to see why, but all we could see was four of the enemy picking up more rocks to throw at us. When the next barrage came, we had to stay down again, and that's when we heard and felt two axes chopping at our wooden legs. We agreed then that things had gotten serious enough for us to bring our cannon into play for the first time ever.

We had put the cannon in one of the portholes and didn't want to move it. We waited until we could see four boys about in line with the cannon and in range. All the time we were hearing and feeling the vibrations from the axes chopping on our supporting posts. In the picture show that morning we had seen that when the soldiers fired the cannon at the Indians they stood back with their hands over their ears. We did this, too, and said to our leader—Hoot Roane or "Buzzard Bill"—the only one of us old enough to carry matches, "Shoot, Hoot."

Hoot lit the powder train that went through the wooden plug in the back of the cannon. The explosion was loud enough to be heard up on the town square, and folks came running to see what we had done this time. There was a blinding flash inside our clubhouse, and the concussion and broken pieces of cast-iron pipe blew the house to bits. The sides blew out, the roof went off, and the floor disappeared. The pieces of cast iron from our blown-up cannon flew around like shrapnel, but miraculously not one of us was hit. We fell the ten feet to the ground—along with what was left of our cannon and rubber guns and hut—right on top of the two boys who had caused it all by trying to chop the legs out from under us. When the smoke and dust cleared away, they left a pile of brush and seven boys trying to get themselves untangled from the trash pile. Nobody was hurt by the explosion; we were just scratched up by the brush.

Brother Will heard the explosion and came over the hill and down to where we were still trying to get out of the mess we had gotten ourselves into. The instant he heard the cannon blow up he knew exactly what had happened and why. He just stood there, not saying anything, and watched us struggle to get out, not helping at all, just looking with a sort of smile on his face and a look in his soft brown eyes that said, "If it hadn't been this, it would have been something else—probably worse, but they've got to learn."

Miss Lillie, the mother of two of our gang, was standing in her kitchen looking out the window when the clubhouse blew up. From the state of peaceful tranquillity that comes on a warm summer Saturday afternoon when all the housework is done except for drying a few more dinner dishes, she went into a state of total fear for her two sons. She had been watching us, and when she saw our clubhouse explode right in front of her eyes she panicked. Knowing that her boys, Shimmy and Cut, were in the middle of all that boiling dust and debris, she dropped the dish she was drying and the drying cloth and jumped out the back door and, holding her ankle-length dress and apron up over her buttoned-up high-top shoes, ran through her garden and pasture as fast as she could, right through briars and weeds. Her eyes wild with fear for her sons, she got to what was left of our clubhouse just as Shimmy and Cut were getting out of the dusty mound of trash. She grabbed both boys by the collar at the back of their necks and, without breaking her stride, turned back up the hill towards her house, pushing them in front of her like a wheelbarrow. As she passed Brother Will she asked, "Mr. Faulkner, how do you raise boys?"

In his calm soft slow voice, Brother Will said, "We don't, Miss Lillie. The Good Lord does."

Brother Will waited for us to get out of the brush pile and then walked in front as we followed him home. He never did fuss at us about it, but he never did fuss at us about anything. He let us find out these things for ourselves, but he was around to help us if we needed him. It wouldn't have done any good to scold us then anyway, because we couldn't hear for three or four days because of the explosion.

About a week later Chooky and Aston Holley and Mac and I were sitting in a glider swing in Brother Will's front yard, and he was sitting close by in one of his wooden lawn chairs reading and about half listening to us. Our hearing had come back by then and we were talking and planning how to build our next clubhouse. I told Chooky and Aston and Mac that when we rebuilt our clubhouse we would have to get a stronger pipe for our cannon.

Brother Will stopped reading then and said, "Don't build any more cannons."

I told him I thought we had used too much powder and that the next time we would use just one croquet ball and put croker sacks full of sand on top of the cannon to hold it in place better.

He said, "I know what you did and how you did it. Now, don't make any more cannons of any kind. You may not blow up just your clubhouse next time, but the whole town as well. But," he added, "come to think about it, that might not be such a bad idea after all for some parts of it."

# First Guns

THE CHRISTMAS TREE sat in the corner of the living room, towering almost to the old high ceilings and spreading out at the bottom to fill that part of the room. It was tied at the top to both walls to keep it from falling off the stand made of crossed pieces of wood picked up from some scrap lumber pile. Lint cotton from the downtown gin that had been running since cotton picking time covered the floor under the tree and was piled against the trunk to make it look like white soft snow. The tree was decorated with strings of white popcorn draped in circles around it on the ends of the branches. Popcorn balls about the size of oranges and brown from the molasses that held the popcorn together hung from the limbs. A few red crepe-paper bells hung high in the tree, and others were hanging around the house on light fixtures and in the tops of doorways. Dolly and Nannie, my mother and my grandmother, cut strips from red and green and yellow and blue paper and glued the ends together to make colored paper chains that reached from branch to branch of the tree like colored ropes.

The fresh woodsy evergreen fragrance that comes along

with cedar trees and their juniper berries filled the room and even drifted up the stairs where my father and mother, Chooky, my little brother who would have his first birthday in another two months, and I lived. And that was across the wide hall that separated our two rooms from the big room and sleeping porch where William, who was Brother Will to me, and Dean, my two uncles who loved little boys, stayed.

Big Dad, the man of the house, and Nannie, the lady of the house (small in stature but so strong in personality that just her wish or desire was a command that was obeyed not only by the family but by all those in her circle of friends and acquaintances without even a thought of saying no to her), stayed in the bedroom downstairs in the big red brick house.

Mistletoe that John, my father, had shot out of the trees in the woods with his .22-caliber rifle hung by red ribbons from the doorways and the light fixtures in the living room and dining room. The dark green leaves spreading around the clusters of white pearl-like berries invited anyone to stand under them and wait for the traditional embarrassing motherly or fatherly Christmas kiss.

John was in civil engineering school at Ole Miss and just a few months away from graduation and Brother Will was getting well into his writing career. Dean, the youngest of the four Falkner brothers, was in school at the university and hunting and playing baseball and golf, probably much more of this than school work. If he didn't get to hunt at least six days out of every week during hunting season—and sometimes out of season, too—he considered it a bad week. He and his bird dogs, Mac and Van, knew the location of every covey of quail in Lafayette County and the neighboring counties as well.

Dean was a great athlete and outdoorsman and such a

good golfer and rifle shot that folks said he was the only person they knew who could play a round of golf with just one golf club, a number two iron, and a .22-caliber rifle and beat par at golf and shoot his limit of squirrels all at the same time. He didn't shoot the squirrels themselves; he barked them. That's shooting the limb right in front of a squirrel's nose so that the bark off the limb or tree knocks him out and the bullet doesn't tear him up.

Brother Will was a good hunter, too, but not as determined as Dean. In fact, all of the Falkner boys were good hunters and fishermen. Guns and dogs and ponies, then horses and hunting and fishing had been part of their lives since they were big enough to ride in front of Big Dad on his horse or tag along after him in the woods and fields while he hunted or fished. When a boy in our family is six years old he gets an air rifle, then a .22-caliber rifle at eight, a .410-gauge shotgun at ten, and finally a 12-gauge shotgun at twelve. As he gets each one, he is taught to hunt with it.

My uncle Jack, the brother between William and John, was away from home. He had been in the Marine Corps during World War I, had been wounded in France, and had come back and finished law school at Ole Miss, but he was away again in the FBI. Brother Will still had his Royal Air Force (Canada) uniform from the war hanging in his closet, along with charts that he had drawn and tacked on the back of the door so he could keep track of where he had sent stories and wouldn't send them to the same place twice. He would let me wear his Sam Browne belt while I played in his room, even though he had to shorten it by tying knots in it to keep it from dragging on the floor and tripping me; in fact, he and Dean would both play with me and let me do anything I wanted to, up to and including shooting Dean's 12-gauge shotgun out an

37

upstairs window. But Nannie put a stop to that. It just didn't set well with the neighbors and the campus authorities. Our closest neighbors were Dr. Bell and Judge Kimbrough. When they were walking to or from their offices on the campus and got close to our house, they would look at the upstairs windows to see if they could see a shotgun. Whether they did or not, they would put a book or something over their heads and hurry to get inside their houses as soon as they could. Brother Will and Dean never did tell them we were just shooting blanks.

That Christmas was about the first one I would be old enough to remember. The Santa Claus parade in Memphis is always a big attraction for children all over the mid-South. We didn't have one in a little town like Oxford, so we had to go to Memphis to see it. John and Dolly and Brother Will and Linda, a cousin of Dolly's, took me to see the Christmas parade in Memphis that year and to do some shopping at the same time.

In those days the seventy-five miles of road between Oxford and Memphis were at best bad, but in the winter they were mostly mud and just plain awful. The family would start getting the car ready the afternoon before we were to leave early the next morning, loading it with jacks, spare tires, patching for punctured tubes, hand air pumps, ropes, axes, and everything else that it might take to get us to the Peabody Hotel in Memphis the same day that we left Oxford. At least two flat tires would have to be fixed on the road, and the car would get stuck in one or two mud holes. We would then have to cut saplings to put under the wheels or find somebody with a team of mules to pull us out. The trip could take from six to eight hours, depending upon the number of mishaps we encountered. A round trip to Memphis wasn't made in just one day, except during the summer, when the days were long and the roads were supposed to be dry and passable; we would spend the night at the Peabody before the return trip.

The cars didn't have heaters, so the night before we left John put bricks in the hot coals in the fireplace to heat all night. The last thing he did before we got in the car at four o'clock the next morning (still over two hours till daylight) was take the hot bricks out of the fire, wrap them in blankets to hold the heat longer, and put them on the floor of the car to keep our feet warm.

We made it to within twenty-five miles of Memphis with only one flat tire, a blowout, and getting stuck once. When the bricks cooled off after four hours, we had to stop in a small country store just inside the Mississippi–Tennessee state line to reheat them on the stove and to get ourselves warm before we made the last leg of the trip that took about two hours to the Peabody. Once we were on the brick streets of Memphis, things went better except for one more flat tire, and that wasn't hard to fix because we were on a hard-surface street and not the mud we had had earlier.

We made it to the Peabody in time for John and Dolly and Linda to do some of their Christmas shopping while Brother Will sat with me in the big lobby and watched the Peabody ducks, the trademark of that famous old hotel, play in the fountain. Then the Christmas parade came down Union Avenue and went by the front door of the Peabody. John and Brother Will took turns holding me up in their arms or on their shoulders so that I could see Santa Claus and all of the parade over the heads of the people who lined the sidewalk. Later we went to a department store so that I could sit on Santa's lap. The stores stayed open on Main Street in Memphis till late at night from Thanksgiving till Christmas, so we looked at all the colorful decorations and toys (mostly toys) before going back to the hotel for a good night's sleep to be ready to tackle that long muddy cold trip back to Oxford the next day. We left long before noon to ensure our getting home by dark.

Everybody in the family got together to have a big Christmas and Santa Claus for me that year. They were just as eager to get the toys out and watch me play with them as I was to get up and see what Santa had left under the tree and in the red and white stocking with bells on the toe that Dolly had made for me to hang on a nail in the mantel over the fireplace.

Each night when John put me to bed he would get me to put my hands up with all my fingers spread so he could touch each one with his trigger finger. He would count from my thumb on one hand and touch each finger from one to nine then Christmas would be the tenth. As we got closer to Christmas Day, it would move nearer to the thumb on my right hand. Finally, the last night, Christmas would be on the thumb and that was the night not to sleep. But John said that I had to sleep so Santa Claus could come. He had written a letter to Santa Claus for me with a drawing of each toy. He put the letter up the chimney and let the draft from the heat of the fire take the letter up and out to the North Pole.

I didn't sleep much that night and John and Dolly gave up sleeping, too, answering my questions: "Has Santa Claus come yet?" or "How much longer do I have to stay in bed?" So we got up. John got up first to go downstairs and wake Nannie and Big Dad. He figured that three o'clock in the morning was just too early to wake Brother Will and Dean, so he let them sleep.

It was a Christmas to remember. It looked like Santa Claus had brought me one of everything, and we tried to play with it all at once—John and Big Dad and I did. Nannie and Dolly just sat on the sofa and watched us playing on the floor. By daylight they were all worn out except me, when Brother Will and Dean finally came down the stairs. Brother Will was in front, holding out what looked like a curtain rod wrapped in just plain old brown wrapping paper. In fact, I really thought it was a curtain rod; and when he handed it to me, I told him that I didn't want a curtain rod. He just grinned, not much with his lips; Brother Will never did grin much that way, but he grinned with his eyes, and that was what he was doing when he said, "Go ahead and open it."

John and Dolly and Nannie and Big Dad watched, too, because they didn't know what it was either. If they had, I wouldn't have gotten it. Anyway, I worked with the paper wrapping (Brother Will never was good at wrapping packages) and finally peeled it back. There was a shiny new Daisy air rifle, my first real shooting gun. John and Big Dad caught their breath, then got mad at Brother Will for giving me a gun when I was only five years old; Dolly and Nannie just looked sick. Brother Will kept on grinning, and so did Dean. Brother Will, Dean, and I were the only ones happy about it. We went outside right then, and they began teaching me how to shoot and be safe with it.

When John settled down and resigned himself to my having the air rifle, he figured that it would be better to join us rather than oppose us, so he helped with my gun training. He taught me what to shoot and what not to shoot. From then on, except for a few brief times, guns have been a big part of my life. That morning, after we got around to loading the chamber with BBs, they went through teaching me how to hold the rifle to my shoulder, sight down the barrel to align the sights on a target, and pull the trigger. I had good teachers.

There were two kinds of birds that I could hunt and shoot

with my air rifle, in addition to the rats and snakes that were out in our barn. One was a jaybird. Dolly always called them "those pesky bluejays." They are just blue crows and will eat everything in the garden before it can be picked. I feel like we are sharecropping with jaybirds in our garden even now, and they make so much noise and are so mean that pretty song-birds won't stay around where they are. Dolly said she had always heard that "jaybirds go to hell on Friday," but she said she didn't believe that; at least, ours didn't go there, because she never did miss them. I could shoot those in our garden.

The other bird that I could shoot was the English sparrow. Horses and mules were tied to the hitching rails around the courthouse on the town square every day then, and there were big oak trees in the courthouse yard. They say that the only two things that can live as cheaply as one are a horse and a sparrow. I guess that's why all the sparrows roosted in the trees every night after the horses and mules had gone home and waited for them to come back to town the next morning after a good healthy breakfast of oats and corn. We couldn't walk under the trees after the hundreds of sparrows had gone to roost about first dark every night for fear of coming out from under the trees with a messy head, so I could shoot those, too.

I hunted in the backyard and garden every day with John and Brother Will helping and overseeing. I didn't hit many birds, but I kept them moving so much with whistling BBs that they didn't get a chance to eat very much out of our winter garden.

They didn't have to worry long about me with the Daisy air rifle, though. The first warm day Dolly put Chooky out in the yard in his playpen. I was out there, too, with my BB gun. Dolly had to go in the house for a minute, and while she was gone I shot up in one of the trees a couple of times. Dolly came running back and took the air rifle away from me, because she thought I was shooting at Chooky. Really I wasn't. I couldn't have hit him anyway; he was hiding behind a pillow.

Three years went by after the Christmas of the Daisy air rifle. By then I was eight years old and Brother Will and Aunt Estelle had gotten married at the College Hill Presbyterian Church in the little community of College Hill about six miles northwest of Oxford. For about a year they lived in an apartment in Miss Elma Meek's house on the street that runs from the town square in Oxford to the university while Brother Will worked nights at the power plant at Ole Miss shoveling coal and writing *As I Lay Dying* on a wheelbarrow that he turned upside down and made into a desk. He could feed coal into the furnace all night long to keep the steam up and write a chapter in his book and still be as clean when he finished as he had been when he came to work twelve hours earlier. Then he bought the old Shegog place, Rowan Oak, which he would call home for the rest of his life.

My father had graduated from Ole Miss. While he was getting established in civil engineering, he moved our family into a house that he had rented just across a pasture from Brother Will's house. Aunt Estelle had a son, Malcolm, about my age from her former marriage. We called him Mac. He and I played together at Rowan Oak out in the front yard, where we climbed the big magnolia and cedar trees and the vines that grew on them and acted the way Tarzan did in the movies we were seeing then, swinging on the grapevines until I fell out of one and landed in the middle of a big briar patch that was so thick I couldn't move. Brother Will had to run from his typewriter and pull me out. That stopped the Tarzan-playing.

Both Mac and I had horses that we rode in Bailey's Woods

(which eventually became University Woods). Bailey's Woods adjoined both our property and Brother Will's place and went west all the way to the railroad tracks that run between Oxford and Ole Miss. Brother Will rode his horses along paths and two or three wagon roads that ran through the woods. In fact, just a few days before he died he was riding his new horse, Stonewall, over by the old ice plant— where he and his brothers and friends had a swimming hole that was kept full of cold water from the plant—when he was thrown from the horse against a red clay bank and hurt his back. This is where we rode, sometimes with Brother Will, but mostly the two of us rode our horses and hunted and fought Indians there. That was one of the times that Brother Will had just gotten back from Hollywood, where he had been writing for the movie people. Mac and I knew that California was even farther west than Texas and that it was where the real cowboys like Tom Mix and Buck Jones and Hoot Gibson were, cowboys we saw in the movies every Saturday morning. We wanted Brother Will to bring us each some chaps and a cowboy hat, and he did. He brought us real leather chaps and two ten-gallon black hats, each with a high peaked crown just like the one that Tom Mix wore, except ours were black with a white band on them. These were like the ones the bad guys in the movies wore. I guess Brother Will figured it was appropriate.

I didn't wear shoes any more than I had to in the summertime. Even for Sunday school, dressed in short pants and white shirt and tie, I could go barefoot as long as my feet were clean. Usually I had a stubbed toe with a big bandage so I couldn't have put on a shoe anyway. John laughed at me for wearing all my cowboy clothes, even the spurs he had given me strapped on my bare feet, while I was riding my horse

44

Button. John said that he bet no cowboy out West ever rode his horse hell-for-leather through mesquite and cactus with his bare toes sticking through the stirrups leading the way like I did through the weeds in our woods and pasture.

That summer John and Brother Will decided we needed pistols to complete our western outfits, and they ordered each of us a .22-caliber pistol in which we were supposed to shoot only blank cartridges. The cartridges had to be a special order, so they bought five hundred at a time each for Mac and me. They taught us how to load and fire the pistols and how to use them safely. When the pistols were fired, a small cap and felt wad and a flame of burning powder came out of the end of the barrel, and it could hurt and burn if somebody was standing too close to the business end of the pistol. With the new gun belts and holsters for our shiny pistols strapped around us and with the rest of our Western garb on, we were real cowboys, although still in short pants and barefooted.

Button was trained for bird hunting, so shooting close to him didn't bother him at all. He was just as calm when I shot in the saddle as when he was eating corn and oats in his stall. But I found out that Mac's horse, Patch, would spook and shy and buck or run away when one of our pistols was fired close to him, so anytime I could get close enough to Mac while he was on Patch I'd shoot, just to see Mac try to keep from falling off while holding on to his ten-gallon hat at the same time. He got so he wouldn't ride close to me while I had my pistol strapped on my side.

When we found a group of Indians we would dismount and chase them on foot because of Patch's tendency to run away or buck if we shot our pistols close to him. We would chase Indians and shoot till all the bad ones had been killed or until one of us stepped on a thorn or stubbed a toe. Then the chase

45

was over till we could go home and get some iodine and a bandage.

We fought Indians around Rowan Oak, too. A good place to get besieged was in the old brick house in the backyard where Brother Will smoked hams and shoulders and sausage. We could always cut off a small sliver of meat and eat it while we were holding off the attacking Indians. Another good place was the log stable where Brother Will kept his horse and milk cow. The first time we shot close to the cow, she bolted and ran. By the time we got her back, with Brother Will's help, after a long chase through the woods and breaking the pasture fence twice (once going out and once coming back in), she was jumpy and skittish and wouldn't give much milk, so after that we had to wait till she was out in the pasture before we could use the stable and loft as a fort to fight off Indians.

Brother Will had a small bull calf out of his milk cow that he kept tied to a long rope to graze in his side yard outside the window of the room where he wrote. We knew that cowboys rode bulls in rodeos, and this bull was just our size. I was the first one to try to ride him. I had on my chaps and cowboy hat and wore spurs on my bare feet. Mac held the bull's head while I straddled his back. We left him on his grazing rope so he wouldn't run far, because I didn't have a bridle or anything to guide him with. I reached for my hat to slap him with like I had seen Tim McCoy and Tom Mix do. I swung the hat and spurred him just as he ran over Mac and we hit the end of the grazing rope. The bull stopped, but I didn't. It wasn't my bare toes that led the way this time—it was my nose and head. I was just getting up and brushing off the grass and other mess that can be found around grazing cattle when Brother Will came running out to see what we had done to his bull calf. Mac wasn't hurt much, just run over and dusty and dirty.

Brother Will thought what we were doing was more interesting right then than his typewriter, so he stayed and helped us. He suggested that we leave off our hats because they were more a hindrance than a help and they wouldn't stay on past the first jump anyway. He told me that I didn't need spurs to make the bull go either. What I really needed was something to make me stop at the same time he did. I told Brother Will that the bull wouldn't have stopped and thrown me if that grazing rope hadn't been tied to him, and Brother Will said, "Yes, but we would still be trying to find you and that bull down in the woods if y'all hadn't been hitched to something." So I took the spurs off.

He helped us catch the bull again and found a leather strap and buckled it around the bull's chest just behind his front legs and over his back to give us something to hold on to. We untied his grazing rope, since I had the strap around him and had a good grip on it, and I knew that by the time I finished this ride that he would be well broken and that we could handle him without any trouble.

While Brother Will and Mac held him, I got well seated, holding on to the strap with both hands, and stuck my bare feet through the strap around his chest and told them to turn him loose. The bull started running and bucking as soon as he knew he was free, and we went down across the yard toward the same big briar patch that I had fallen into while playing Tarzan. The strap was so tight that my feet were caught and I couldn't turn loose with my hands. We went through that briar patch at a full gallop, with my bare toes leading the way.

Just the other side of the briar patch was a low hanging loop of one of the big grapevines that we had used as our

47

Tarzan vine. It caught me under my chin and around my neck and jerked me off the bull's back in spite of the strap holding my hands and feet. The vine had stretched some and bent the limb to which it was attached. When my hands and feet slipped out of the strap, the limb and vine snapped back in place, flipping me right back into the middle of the same briar thicket.

Brother Will and Mac came running, and Brother Will waded through the briars to pull me out again. He was laughing in his chuckling sort of way, so hard that tears were rolling down his cheeks. I didn't think it was so funny this time either, just as I hadn't thought it was funny when I fell in that same briar thicket playing Tarzan. My throat hurt from that vine, besides all the stickers in me and the scratches that they had made. Brother Will said I looked as if I'd been shot out of a slingshot backwards and upside down and that after I had been tossed in the briar patch, he could just see my bare toes sticking out above the tops of the briars. He looked at my skinned and vine-burned neck and said it looked like somebody had tried to hang me. I told him that bull *had*. He said that we were going to wear out that briar patch just pulling me out of it.

That summer we moved into the big house on University Avenue with my other grandparents, Dolly's mother and father, while John was surveying right-of-way for the Mississippi State Highway Department for a road between Greenwood and Clarksdale. He came in every Friday night and left again Sunday night. It was the house that he later bought from Dolly's father for us to live in as our own and there he spent his last twenty-some years writing and painting. It backed up to Bailey's Woods on the north side and Brother Will's property backed up to it on the south, so I could ride Button through the woods and be at Rowan Oak in just a few minutes.

Mac and I shot bad Indians at Brother Will's house all that summer. He didn't mind the shooting. In fact, he had such a power of concentration that he could block out everything that was going on around him anyway.

One cloudy, not quite rainy afternoon that September while I was visiting Nannie, my grandmother Falkner, she decided that she wanted to see Brother Will about something and asked me if I'd like to go down with her to see him. I had my trusty pistol with me but couldn't shoot it around Nannie's house, and I thought there might be some more bad Indians that I could shoot, so I said that I would. As soon as we got to my uncle's house, Nannie went in to see Brother Will and I went to the stable to resume my war on rampaging Indians. I was fighting a whole tribe by myself that afternoon because Mac had gone to town with his mother to get a haircut. The war got boring and I decided to go inside to see what Nannie and Brother Will were doing.

Rowan Oak at that time had a porch or gallery that ran all the way across the back of the library and hall and along the west side of the dining room and kitchen, with a door going into the hall. John and Brother Will had preached to me over and over again about gun safety, and one of the rules was never to take a loaded gun in the house. So when I got to the door from the back porch to the hall, I pulled my loaded pistol from its holster. I was going to unload it so I could go in the house without breaking one of Brother Will's rules and accidentally shooting somebody. I held the pistol with my right hand, placed my left hand firmly on top of the barrel, and with my right thumb drew the hammer back. The hammer and barrel were slick with moisture from the high humidity. As I put pressure on the barrel to break it open in the middle so that I could take out the live cartridge, my hand slipped over the end of the barrel just as my thumb slipped off the hammer. The explosion of the pistol shot was deafening, compounded by the sound bouncing off the wooden walls and floor and ceiling of the back porch, making me feel like I was in an echo box. But that wasn't nearly as bad as the numbness and the burning hurt where all the wadding and burning powder went into my hand. The pistol clattered to the floor when I grabbed my blackened hand, which was spurting blood. The porch echoed with my scream and the slam of the screen door against the wall as Brother Will ran out with Nannie right behind him to see what had happened to me this time. The second he saw me, he knew. He went to the bathroom, got a towel, and wrapped my hand in it; then he and Nannie took me to Dr. Ashford Little's office, which was upstairs over Gathright-Reed's Drug Store on the square.

Dr. Little was a young and upcoming doctor in our town and was later to become a real friend, but for a time after this I had my doubts about that, since he didn't believe in any kind of painkiller, especially for somebody careless enough to shoot himself. He picked most of the powder out of my hand with me sitting there watching and hurting and crying and wishing it had happened to anybody else but me. Brother Will stood on one side of the chair in which Dr. Little had put me with my swollen, bleeding hand turned up on the table under a strong light so he could see and pick out the grains of burned powder and felt wadding with his pointed tweezers. Nannie stood on the other side with her consoling hand on my shoulder, flinching every time I did. When he was through,

*Yours Respectfully*

*W. C. Falkner*

Colonel W. C. Falkner

John W. T. Falkner

Sallie Murry
Williams, and
Holland Wilkins

John Faulkner

Maud Falkner

John Faulkner home, Oxford

Dean Faulkner,
brother of
William Faulkner

Nan Faulkner

John Faulkner and William Faulkner

Murry Falkner, Malcolm Franklin, and Jim Faulkner

Jim Faulkner, Dean Faulkner, Murry Falkner,
Malcolm Franklin, and Jill Faulkner

Jim Faulkner

the pain wasn't gone from the pistol shot, but that was just a dull throb compared to the sharp pain of the tweezers.

Dr. Little cleaned up the mess, wrapped my hand in a ball of white gauze about the size of a grapefruit, and put a sling around my neck to hold my arm level with my stomach so that blood wouldn't run to my hand and make it throb. Then he thought he was through—but he wasn't. Brother Will said to Dr. Little, "Now, Ashford, we are going to take him home to Lucille." That's what he called my mother, Dolly. "John's not here. He's surveying some road over in the Delta so the people can drive up and down it and ruin our hunting."

Not being too sure of himself in a confrontation with Dolly, Dr. Little told Brother Will, "No, Bill, I'd rather stay here."

In his soft firm voice, knowing that his wishes would be carried out, Brother Will said, "Ashford, you and Mother and I will take him home to his mother. You can explain this better than I can."

Dr. Little didn't argue. He just said, "All right, let's go and get this over with." He didn't want to face Dolly, but he didn't want to say no to Brother Will either, so we all got in Brother Will's car and went to see my mother.

As we walked up the steps and across the porch to the front door I could see Dolly standing in the hall watching us. Brother Will opened the door and gently pushed me inside, then with his hand on Nannie's elbow ushered her in, too. Dolly looked at me, then down at my hand, and asked, "What's happened to you now?"

Brother Will turned to Dr. Little, who was holding back some, and said, "Now, Ashford, you go in and tell her about it." Wanting to get the explanation over with, Dr. Little wasn't very gentle or tactful. He blurted out, "Lucille, I'm

51

going to do all I can to save his hand." And with that he turned and left, Nannie and Brother Will right behind him, leaving me to explain to Dolly how I came to shoot myself in the hand. Dolly stood there a minute, somewhat taken aback by Dr. Little's abrupt statement. Then she took the note that he had given me telling us how to care for my hand till it got well.

By Thanksgiving, two and a half months later, my hand was as good as new, but Brother Will hadn't been around since that September afternoon when they brought me home, even though it was just a few hundred yards between the back of our properties. The morning of the day after Thanksgiving he drove up our driveway and came in the house and told me that he wanted to take me to town and buy a new suit for me. I said, "Fine, I'd like to have one." We went to town, just Brother Will and me, to Mr. Rocky Webster's clothing store, and when we got to the racks that held all the little boys' suits, he said, "Rocky, he can have any suit in the house, as long as it doesn't have a pistol pocket in it."

# Solo

I N GOOD OLD LAZY OXFORD during the summers in
the early 1930s children made their own entertainment,
and just living and being contented were the main interests. It was a good time for little boys still a few years away
from their teens yet, playing in the woods and around Rowan
Oak. Brother Will, my uncle, had bought his home just two
or three years before; and with part of an advance payment
from MGM, he bought a Waco Cabin airplane. He kept it in
Memphis because there was a hangar to protect it from the
weather when it was on the ground, and the flying field was
larger. Captain Vernon Omlie was there to look after it and to
help Brother Will get back into flying after having been away
from aviation since his flying days in Canada during World
War I.

Oxford had only a small cow pasture flying field occasionally used by some lost or barnstorming pilot who would be
met by curious people, usually Brother Will or John among
them, who would many times bring them to town for a good
meal and a night's rest before a show or going on to another
town the next day.

One day that summer Brother Will took four of us, Chooky (my little brother), Malcolm (his stepson), and Arthur Guyton (a friend of ours), and me to Memphis to spend the day at the airport flying in his airplane. That was the first plane ride I ever had, and Brother Will was the pilot; but it wasn't the first time I had ever flown, or at least not the first time I had ever been in the air without my feet touching the ground for just a few seconds anyway.

John, my father, and Brother Will had always been interested in flying, and sometimes on Sunday afternoons we would go to air shows put on by barnstorming pilots close to Oxford. We watched one or two airplanes take passengers up on sight-seeing rides over town for a dollar apiece. The rides were about ten minutes long, and the crowd would strain their eyes looking for the returning airplane. After it landed and taxied up in front of the crowd, the wind-blown passenger heroes, exhilarated by the flight because they had braved the perils of being detached from the ground, would get out of the passenger cockpit and step down from the wing of the plane amid the joking remarks of people who had not flown yet. They would then join the crowd to wait for the last event of the day—the parachute jump.

The jumper, who came along with the pilots in one of the planes, sold tickets for rides until time for the jump; then with great ceremony he would strap on his parachute and an emergency parachute (called a chest pack) while answering questions from big-eyed little boys. He would climb in the plane and wave to the people as he and the pilot taxied out for takeoff. The plane would climb in a slow lazy circle around the field till it was the right altitude and upwind of the field so the jumper, after his parachute opened, could drift with the wind and land in front of the people on the ground. At first all

54

we could see would be a small dot falling away from and behind the plane. Someone in the crowd would yell, "There he is!" and everybody would look and get real quiet, watching the falling body growing larger and falling farther behind the plane. The longer the parachute jumper delayed pulling the rip cord that opened the parachute, the stiller and quieter the crowd became. Some of them were probably waiting to see a tragedy, others to see something new and experience the thrill of a free-fall with a rescue by the parachute. When the white silk streamed up from the falling man and blossomed, jerking him back from his rapid descent and setting him in a gentle swaying motion slowly approaching the ground, the crowd would let out a collective sigh and some would say, "Nobody could pay me to do that." Then usually a group of boys would run out to gather around the jumper when he touched the ground and help him collect and fold up his now collapsed parachute. The jumpers made a hundred dollars a jump, paid out of the gate receipts.

We had an air show in Oxford one Sunday afternoon that summer on a field just south of town that was more of a cow pasture than an airfield. Brother Will had asked some of his flying friends in Memphis to put on the show—stunt planes, parachute jumper, and all. When the time came for the jump, Navy Sowell (he rode a motorcycle through a flaming wall, too, trying to draw more spectators) jumped from the plane after the ritual of putting on his parachutes in front of the small crowd, and he delayed his parachute opening just right and landed in front of the people amid cheers and applause.

There wasn't enough money from the gate to pay the advertising let alone pay Navy a hundred dollars for making the jump and gathering the small crowd so that barnstorming pilots could sell their sight-seeing rides for a dollar, so a hat

55

was passed among the spectators for donations. When the hat came back, it contained only a few quarters, dimes, and nickels. Brother Will, seeing this and feeling responsible in a way and sorry for Navy, put in a ten-dollar bill, probably the last one he had.

These parachute jumpers were the drawing cards that attracted the crowd so that the barnstorming pilots could sell sight-seeing rides. Since they were the main attraction, they were always trying something new to bring more people to the show. One man named Irvin Davis made what he called bat wings that he could use to control his flight or fall some before opening his parachute. He had a one-piece coverall with long sleeves to which he had attached a strong piece of canvas-like fabric from under each arm all the way down both sides to his ankles and under his arms out to his wrists. The same kind of cloth filled the space between his legs so that with his legs spread and his arms stretched straight out like he was standing spread-eagled he was a solid sheet of fabric. He looked like a flying squirrel spread out to glide from one tree to another. I watched Irvin Davis jump during an air show one Sunday afternoon, and from where I stood on the ground it seemed as if he sailed for a long time before he finally opened his parachute and floated to the ground.

Right then I decided that was for me. If Irvin Davis, weighing two hundred pounds, could fly as he had just done, I reasoned that since I weighed only fifty or sixty pounds I wouldn't need a parachute to make an easy soft landing. I could do it with my own bat wings.

I remembered that I had seen some heavy canvas or sailcloth while I was playing in one of the storerooms in the old brick building in the backyard at Brother Will's house. It would be just right for my bat wings, and the stable in his horse lot would be high enough for me to run along the ridge of the tin roof, jump, and fly. It took me about a week to measure and cut the wings out of the canvas with my dull hunting knife. I used the car tire innertube rubber bands that we had made for our rubber gun wars to attach them to a pair of coveralls that we called unionalls. I couldn't work on them all the time because Brother Will walked around the yard sometimes and I didn't want him to know that I was cutting my wings out of his good sailcloth. He wouldn't have taken too kindly to that until he saw me flying; then he would think it was fine.

When I finished the flying suit I tried it on in the barn, being careful that Brother Will didn't see me, and stood with my bare feet as far apart as the canvas sailcloth between my legs would allow and my arms straight out, spread-eagled just as I had seen Irvin Davis do that day at the air show. Chooky, my little brother, said I looked just like Davis.

I was ready for my solo flight. I told Chooky that the first time we found Brother Will sitting in his front yard in the afternoon as he usually did I was going to put on my flying suit, run along the ridge of the stable, dive off the end nearest to our uncle, and launch myself with enough speed to fly over his head and surprise him. Then I would sail back to the barn and land. Then he, Chooky, could use my suit to see if he could fly like me.

I could visualize myself sailing gracefully like a hawk that I had seen soaring and circling lazily over our chickens waiting for a chance to dive on them and catch one for his dinner. It looked so easy the way he did it, not even flapping his wings, that I knew I could do it too.

We were playing around the stable one afternoon a few days later when Brother Will walked out to the front yard to relax in one of the wooden lawn chairs that he kept in the shade of the trees. I told Chooky to watch for me while I put on my bat wing flying suit and climbed to the roof of the stable. He was then to stand in front of Brother Will, facing me, and talk to him. When I was in the middle of my takeoff run to make my solo flight, Chooky would point to me and say, "Look, Brother Will. Watch him fly."

It wasn't easy to climb the ladder in back of the stable with my flying suit on because the canvas sailcloth between my legs and between my legs and arms restricted my step and reach. I made it to the roof without Brother Will seeing me, but I couldn't stay up there long because the summer sun had been bearing down on it all day long and it was so hot that my bare feet couldn't stay in one place more than about a second without my picking them up one at a time to cool the bottoms. So I had to start my takeoff run as soon as I saw Chooky in position in front of Brother Will. My stride was shortened because of the canvas sailcloth between my legs, but I ran as fast as I could, taking short steps along the ridge of the roof toward the end closest to where Brother Will was sitting and listening to Chooky. When I was so close to the end of the roof that I couldn't have stopped had I wanted to, I saw Chooky point to me and Brother Will turn around to see where he was pointing.

Brother Will dropped the book he had been reading when Chooky interrupted him, jumped up, and yelled, "WHOA, STOP, JIM, DON'T, LOOK OUT," and came running to catch me or be there when I landed.

I was glad he turned around when he did, because now he could see my entire flight from the beginning, when I leaped and sailed from the stable roof out over his head, to the end, when I came back and landed by the stable where Chooky would be waiting to take his turn at flying. I reached the end of my takeoff run and made a big flat spread-eagled dive like doing a belly-buster in the swimming hole in the creek just about the time he took his first step toward me. I could see myself soaring out over his head. I was spread out in what I had imagined was my flying position, but I didn't see the grass in the backyard slowly drifting by under me as I sailed across the lawn toward Brother Will's upturned amazed and admiring face. I was airborne all right, but not in the flat graceful glide I had imagined. I was in a head-first straight-down dive like a dive bomber, headed toward the ground and a green hedge bush that grew about ten feet out from the stable. It came rushing up at me so fast that I didn't even have time to put my arms and hands in front of me before I hit the bush headfirst like a bomb released from a dive bomber. I felt and heard the limbs and leaves scratching and breaking as I went right through the middle from the top almost to the bottom. What stopped me and prevented me from actually making contact with the ground—and probably breaking my neck—was a big limb that broke off. The stub stuck through the canvas sailcloth between my legs, stopped me with a shock-absorber effect from the big rubber bands with which I had attached the wings, and held me dangling upside down a few feet above the ground like a sleeping bat that I guess it looked like I was trying to imitate. I wasn't hurt, except for my pride, but the hedge was badly mangled.

Brother Will lifted me off the stub of the limb, set me upright, and brushed me off to see if I was all right. "Jim," he said, "if you don't stop these crazy stunts, you are going to break up every bush on the place."

I told him that I didn't think I was going fast enough when I came off the roof. He just said, "Don't try that again, and stay out of the bushes. We don't have many left now after you and this summer." Then he added, "If you just *have* to fly, get Chooky and Mac and Art Guyton and we'll go to Memphis tomorrow and do some flying; but don't jump off that barn again."

We were up at daylight the next morning, and the four of us, with Brother Will and Dean, his youngest brother, went to the Memphis airport and spent the day flying in his airplane. We took turns flying with him, and I was the first to go up with him piloting. When we came down, our landing was a lot easier than mine had been the day before in my bat wing flying suit into that hedge on my first solo flight off the barn.

# Saturday Night at the Pelican

OUR FARM, GREENFIELD, is about seventeen miles east of Oxford on Puskus Creek in Beat Two, Lafayette County, Mississippi. Back in the 1930s the road out our way had just been graveled, and it was the only graveled road around. The others were still dirt, so we called this one "The Rock." If people wanted to go to town they had to pick a dry sunny day because there was a mile of dirt road across Puskus Creek bottom from Greenfield to the Rock. Our mile of road has been graveled now, but then it was dirt, or worse than that when it rained—just pure mud. After they reached the Rock, they would catch a ride with someone passing by in a wagon or truck. Very few people had cars back then, not because cars weren't plentiful but because money was scarce, and there just wasn't all that much need for transportation other than going to town three or four times a year. In the spring before planting some folks had to make arrangements with the bank or some merchant in town to furnish them farm supplies and living necessities on credit until the crops were gathered in the fall and settlements could be made. When storekeepers opened their books to farmers in the spring, they called it "opening the Book of Life." Another time for going to town was in the late summer after laying-by time, when there was nothing to do until harvest. Some folks would go to town other than just on Saturdays to gather in the courthouse yard or around the town square and visit with friends from other parts of the county and discuss crops and politics. After all the crops were in, people would go to town to buy things for Christmas and to settle their accounts for the year with the merchants and bankers, so the "Book of Life" could be closed until planting time the next spring. Most of the time they spent on the farm or around the neighborhood with the only entertainment being what they provided for themselves.

The folks who lived and worked at Greenfield and some of our neighbors came to us, or rather to my father and uncle, and asked if they could build a meeting hall or a gathering place somewhere on the farm at Greenfield so that they could get together on Saturdays and other special occasions. That suited us fine as long as it was at the end of the farm away from our house so they wouldn't disturb anybody.

Building the meeting hall turned into a community project. Everyone pitched in and worked, and with a little financial help from us they erected a good-size wooden meeting hall. It was unpainted and unfinished inside, but it was good enough and large enough for meetings and dances and just about any other gathering anyone wanted. The outside walls were made of vertical twelve-inch-wide boards nailed only at the top, so that if the sheriff arrived unexpectedly or things got too rowdy inside, anybody at any place along the wall inside could just push a plank and it would swing outward, opening from the bottom, allowing the person to step outside through the gap. The plank would fall back in place of its own weight, leaving no sign that anyone had just stepped through the wall to escape the danger of being caught or hurt. Thus the whole building could be evacuated by any number of people in just a matter of seconds, leaving the sheriff or the person causing the disturbance all alone in the big room.

They called this building the Pelican for no reason that I know of, except that somebody once said, "It looks jus' like a big ole Pelican," and the name stuck. The Pelican was within walking or horseback riding or wagon riding distance of nearly all the people in our little part of the county, and many other people, too, if they just wanted to go to the Pelican badly enough.

Just as soon as it was completed, things began to happen. Meetings and gatherings took place during the daytime and dances and parties at night. The times when white lightning flowed more freely than other times was when the sheriff had been busy on the other side of the county long enough for the makers to put up a few gallons of corn whiskey to pay for and liven up the coming Saturday night at the Pelican. When corn whiskey was available, it seemed as if somebody just had to get right in the middle of the dance floor and fire a few shots from his newly acquired pistol to show it off and to see if it really would shoot. This action would completely empty the dance hall, leaving the owner of the pistol standing alone in the center of the room with the side planks of the building slamming shut where revelers had just stepped outside to get out of the way of flying bullets.

Little Bango, a son of old Big Man Bango who lived at Greenfield, happened to pick one of these nights to go to the Pelican for the first time. Little Bango was an amiable young fellow, not a very big man and not the kind of person you would expect to enjoy a Saturday night at the Pelican.

Although he seemed much more suited to going to a church social, he wanted to go to the Pelican; so Renzi, a friend of his who also lived at Greenfield, and a few others who were frequent patrons of the dance hall agreed to take him.

That Saturday night they all dressed up in their best clothes and hitched our best team of mules to the wagon. They put cane-bottom chairs on the wagon bed to sit in, so they would have the least amount of dust and dirt on themselves and their clothes when they got to the Pelican. Little Bango was ready first. He stood first on one foot then the other, eager to get to the dance hall and ready to see all the happenings that he had only heard about from Renzi and the other folks who wouldn't let a Saturday night go by without at least passing through the Pelican, even if they were just about two jumps in front of the sheriff and went right on through and out one of the loose planks on the wall. The sheriff said the Pelican was the hardest place in Mississippi to catch a man. At any other place all he had to do was station a deputy at each outside door and that would be it, but at the Pelican he had to put one at every plank around the building.

As they drove into the side yard to tie the mules to a hitching post close to where the earlier arrivals had parked their wagons and tied their horses and mules, Little Bango could hear the banjo and fiddle music and laughter already going strong and giving promise of a real Pelican Saturday night. As the night wore on, the corn whiskey flowed freer and the noise grew louder. Little Bango was standing with his back against the wall watching people on the dance floor and listening to the music when a big fellow named Dime, who had just bought a new Owl Head pistol that day, walked to the middle of the floor, pulled that new pistol out of his pistol pocket, and fired three shots. The crowd scattered like a covey of quail surprised by a hungry fox. Each person ran for the nearest plank in the closest wall to get outside and put something between himself and Dime and that exploding pistol and those flying bullets.

The first shot struck the plank just behind Little Bango about six inches directly above his head. The impact of the bullet helped, but it wasn't really needed for Little Bango to swing the plank out and immediately quit the building. He hit the ground running, not even stopping to wait for Renzi and the others and the wagon; and as he told it, he was gaining speed all the way down the dusty road the two miles to his and Big Man Bango's cabin just across the valley on the next hill from our house. He had scratches all over his face and arms and everywhere else that was exposed to the briars and branches that hung out over the road. Little Bango ran through them at full speed, because it was dark and he couldn't see; but even seeing them and knowing that he was going to hit them wouldn't have slowed him down at all in his state of mind that night.

It was the next morning before we knew anything about the shooting, and Little Bango didn't know till then, either, that Dime's third shot had killed Buster Creel, a mean sort of fellow who lived down Puskus Creek from us. Most of the time Buster was hard to get along with, and we were surprised that he had lived as long as he had without somebody doing him in. Dime didn't really mean to kill Buster; at least, none of us knew of any bad blood between them. It just happened while Dime was showing off his new pistol like folks did sometimes on a bouncing Saturday night at the Pelican.

Nevertheless, it did happen, and Dime had to be tried for it. We all liked Dime and hadn't thought too much of Buster and knew that sooner or later somebody would have to do something about him anyway. So we went to town that Sunday night and asked Uncle John to defend Dime when his case came up in court that fall. Uncle John was really my father's uncle, my great-uncle, but all of us called him Uncle John anyway. He was the best lawyer in Lafayette County and probably in Mississippi. They called him "The Lion of the Courtroom." When he roared, everybody sat back and listened, and he never lost a killing case.

After we had told Uncle John all we knew about the shooting and he had agreed to defend Dime, John, my father, went to the old two-story red brick jailhouse where Dime had been staying since the shooting. John told him that everything was going to be all right and that he was not to worry. John added that we were sure Dime didn't intend to do it and that Uncle John, the best lawyer we knew, was going to defend him. Everything was going to turn out just fine.

Uncle John came from town out to our part of the county a number of times before the trial to talk to the witnesses. As it turned out, Little Bango was one of the few people who had actually seen Dime pull the pistol from his pistol pocket and fire the first shot that hit just above Little Bango's head. Uncle John spent a lot of time with Little Bango getting the story straight and preparing his case.

Little Bango developed, or so he thought, into quite a celebrity among the rest of the folks on the farm, and I remember one day John saying, "I'll be damn glad when that shooting case of Dime's and Little Bango's is over so they can settle down and go back to work." The trial came up in that fall term of court, which was held after the crops had been laid by and before it was time to harvest. Then the farmers and people who worked on farms could serve as jurors or come only as spectators without interfering with their work.

Little Bango had been served his summons papers by

Mister Buddy, our sheriff, and us, too, because we all had to help Mister Buddy serve the papers. Little Bango saw Mister Buddy coming and, like he said, he just had to run when he saw the "High Shurf" coming up the path to his house, even if he hadn't done anything. So he ran out the back door and into the woods behind his smokehouse. We found him and explained to him that this was just the way things like this had to be done, and that he had to have the papers so the county could pay him for being a witness even if it was for Dime and against the county, and that the county officials wouldn't hold it against him for doing it. So Little Bango came out of the woods with us and accepted the summons from Mister Buddy.

The first day of the trial came, and Little Bango was up and dressed in his Sunday-go-to-meeting suit long before first light, anxious to get to town and the courthouse yard well before the trial began so he could walk around among his friends and acquaintances, since he was the star witness. By the time Renzi and James, another fellow on the place who looked after the livestock, had fed the horses and mules, Little Bango was at the barn impatiently pacing back and forth and carefully stepping around the little dust puddles to keep his shoes from being too dirty when he got to town.

After the animals had finished eating, James brought one of the gentlest of the horses from the stable and saddled it for Little Bango to ride the mile across Puskus bottom to the Rock so he could catch an early ride to town and not be late meeting his friends in the courthouse yard before the trial got under way. We were going in later, but Little Bango couldn't wait that long and take the chance of being a little late and miss being the center of attention. I think he would have gone to town the day before, but John just wouldn't hear of it.

Little Bango or anybody else who rode a horse from

Greenfield to the Rock to catch a ride to town would then tie the bridle reins to the saddle horn so they wouldn't drag the ground, and the horse would return to the barn by itself. Little Bango mounted his horse that morning and headed across Puskus Creek to the Rock, a mile away. We heard him cross the wooden bridge over the creek just outside the gate from the home pasture where the barn was; then just a short time later we heard a horse crossing the wooden bridge coming our way. We recognized Little Bango coming through the gate. I thought: The horse wants to come back to the barn and Little Bango can't stop him. But it wasn't the horse that wanted to come back; it was little Bango. He had forgotten his summons.

When Little Bango rode up to where we were standing and told us why he had come back, John told him to stay put and sent Renzi running up the hill to Little Bango's cabin to get the summons. Renzi put the paper in Little Bango's pocket, put him back on the horse, and said, "Boy, you betta git. Mista John an' 'at judge bof gonna sen' you off, ifen you don't git dere on time."

Well, Little Bango did get there in time to spend a few minutes in the courthouse yard with his friends and enjoy his newfound importance before court began. We got there in time for the beginning, too. The first part of the trial dragged along and was boring, with each lawyer trying to develop the case for his side, but when Little Bango was put on the witness stand, things started to pick up. Uncle John had things pretty well in hand and going Dime's way. He had saved Little Bango until last to put the icing on the cake, or maybe just on Dime. Little Bango was big-eyed and scared and squirming around in his seat as Uncle John walked across the courtroom to the witness chair and said in a soft voice, trying to calm him down, "Howdy, Little Bango, how you feelin' today?"

Little Bango sort of relaxed then and grinned up at Uncle John and answered, "Jus' fine, Mista John, an' Ah hopes you is, too."

Uncle John turned around, biting his lip to maintain his composure, then said, "Now, tell the Court what your name is and where you live."

Little Bango cut his eyes up at Uncle John and asked, "Who da Cou't?"

Uncle John nodded toward the judge and said, "That gentleman sitting up there."

Little Bango looked at the judge a minute and said, "Ah do say. Ah thought 'at wuz Mist' An'son from over dere 'bout Ripley, what come to da picnic what our Mist' John give fo' everbody in da summertime a'ter usuns gits done layin'-by da crops."

Uncle John said, "He is, but when he's in here, he's the Court."

Little Bango said, "Ah guess he done change his name den lak Willie B. done when he foun' out who his daddy wuz."

The judge banged his gavel, and Uncle John told Little Bango to stop, so they could get back to what everybody came to hear, about Dime and Buster at the Pelican. Little Bango was looking at the gavel and the place on the bench where the judge had hit. Uncle John said, "Now Little Bango, look here and answer my question."

He looked back at Uncle John and said, "Yassuh, Mist' John, I'se Little Bango. Big Man Bango, he my papa. We stays wid our Mist' John out chere on Puskus Creek."

Little Bango stretched up in the witness chair, trying again to see what the judge had hit with the gavel. The judge banged the gavel twice more to get things back in order, and Uncle John told Little Bango to look back at him so that they could get on with the questions about Dime and Buster. Little Bango, still looking at the gavel, said to Uncle John, "Mist' John, tell Mist' da Cou't dat you can't drive nair nail wid no wooden hammer. Jus' as soon as we gits done here, Ah'll see can Ah fix 'at nail in 'is destie fo' 'im. I'se right handy at fixin' things lak dat."

The judge raised his gavel to bang it again, but looked at Little Bango, then at the gavel, and put it down. He rested his chin in his hand and looked at Uncle John, as if to say, "He's all yours."

Uncle John said, "Now, Little Bango, where were you the Saturday night in question?"

"Which Saddy night wuz 'at what you talkin' 'bout?"

Uncle John was beginning to turn red, his eyes were getting dark, and he looked as if he could wring Little Bango's neck in exasperation. Through his teeth he said, "Every Saturday night all you people out there in Beat Two always gather at least once at the Pelican. No matter what else is happening, even on Judgment Day, if it comes on a Saturday night, you'll ask Him to wait so you can make one more trip through the Pelican."

Uncle John cut his eyes up at the judge, who had just picked up his gavel. The judge looked from Uncle John to Little Bango and back at the gavel, then put it down and returned his chin to rest on his hand. Uncle John looked back at Little Bango, biting his lip to regain his composure, and said, "Little Bango, tell the Court where you were on that Saturday night when Buster got shot at that Pelican place ya'll got out there in Beat Two."

70

"Mist' John, I wuz rat dere in da Pelican; I sho wuz. Is 'at what da Cou't wanta know?"

"YES," Uncle John said, hoping that he had Little Bango back on the right track. "Now, Little Bango, think hard and tell the Court what you saw that night."

Little Bango said, "Mist' John, hit wuz jus' lak Ah tol' you 'at day you come out to where we wuz plowin' jus' south uv de creek. Ah wuz stan'in' rat dere an' seed Dime unshuck 'at gun from outen his pistol pocket." Little Bango's eyes were getting big and excited now, remembering that night, and he kept on: "An' hit warn't no sooner en Ah seed 'at Owl Head come unshucked 'at Ah tol' mah foots 'at we's gonna hafta move."

Uncle John stopped him and said, "Now, Little Bango, tell the Court where you were when the first one of those three shots was fired."

"Mist' John, tell da Cou't hit wuz jus' lak Ah sayed 'at day you wuz out to da farm, Ah was stan'nin' rat dere in 'at same place, an' 'at bullet, hit went rat ova mah haid." He pointed with his right trigger finger just over his head. And he kept on, "Ifen Ah wuz six foot tall lak you is, 'at bullet woulda hit me rat square twix mah eyes." Uncle John was biting his lip again. The judge had his hand over his mouth, but he couldn't keep the tears from running down his cheeks, and his face was turning red.

Uncle John asked, "Little Bango, where were you when the second shot was fired?"

"Mist' John, Ah had done stepped outside by den through one uv dem loose swingin' planks, an' wuz 'bout a hunert yards down da road tow'd home."

Uncle John got serious again because, as he said later, it could look as if there were a time interval between the shots,

71

and it wouldn't look good for Dime. He asked, "Little Bango, where were you when that third shot was fired?"

Little Bango said, "Ah wuz jus' gittin' stretched out good 'bout den, an' Ah wuz jus' turnin' 'at curve dere 'round Uncle Jim's house, 'bout a half a mile down da road. An' you know Mist' John, Ah slud ofen 'at road, outen 'at curve an' down in 'at ditch, but Ah scrootched up mah toes an' clum rat back up outen 'at ditch, an' Ah didn't miss no runnin' lick atall. An' as soon as Ah hit dat flat road agin, Ah wuz home in nothin' flat. Ah wuz up 'bout Uncle Jim's yestiddy an' seed mah toe marks, dey wuz still dere."

The judge had both hands on his face now and even the prosecuting attorney was laughing some, but Uncle John wasn't. He thought this really might be hurting his case because of the time lapse between shots that had let Little Bango run so far and given Dime a chance to think about where that last shot that had killed Buster might go. So he was more than just serious now; he was worried when he asked, "Little Bango, just how fast were those shots fired?"

Little Bango's eyes were big again, and he was excited now, reliving that night when he was trying to get away from all that shooting and killing. He looked up at Uncle John and said about as fast as his lips could move, "Boom-boom-boom, dat what hit sayed, Mist' John, 'at Owl Head pistol, hit sayed boom-boom-boom."

The judge whirled around in his swivel chair, so that his back was to the courtroom. He wasn't making any sound, but his head was bobbing up and down. Uncle John backed up to the table where Dime was sitting. He just leaned there relieved now and chuckling. The sheriff and the county attorney were leaning out the same window. The judge turned around with tears running down his face and banged his

72

gavel, not thinking about Little Bango and the nail this time, to bring the courtroom back to order.

The jury foreman stood up, still holding his side, and said, "Your Honor, we don't have to go out. Not guilty." The judge banged his gavel and said, "Dismissed."

Uncle John said to John, my father, who was sitting just outside the rail, "Get Little Bango and Dime back to Beat Two and keep them there. And, by the way, the Judge and I will be out there tomorrow to see the Pelican and Little Bango's toe marks in that curve around Uncle Jim's house."

# Reading Maps

A BELL CLANGING AT THE BACK DOOR broke the quiet of a lazy summer Sunday afternoon while I was sitting in the kitchen drinking a cup of coffee and trying to wake up from my nap. It had to be Double Dip, because nobody can time my getting up from a nap or anything else the way he can, and nobody can clang that bell like he does, either.

Double Dip and Ammonia live in a house out in the back and down the hill from our house, and they have lived on the place and worked for us for years, even before he had to go to Parchman, the state penitentiary, for a few years because he had to kill Dusty in a crap game that time when Dusty tried to pass the smaller part of a torn dollar bill to him.

Just like always, Ammonia stayed with us while Double Dip was gone; and when he came back from Parchman, it was just like always, too. He came in during the night of the day that they had let him go, and the first time I saw him back was when I looked out the kitchen window before breakfast that morning. There he was at the barn, feeding the horses the way he did every day, and that day, too, seven years before, when he had had to leave with the sheriff.

Double Dip Da Man wasn't the name he was born with (I don't guess anybody remembers his real name, not even him), but it was a name that he sort of carved out of life for himself, and it was the one that he went by now and had for a long time. It was even that way on the rolls down at Parchman. Back when he was growing up, all he ever wanted was a double dip ice cream cone. If he had only a nickel, which would buy a single dip, he would wait till he came across another one some place so that he could afford two dips of ice cream on his cone. He ate so many and got so big that he even looked like a double dip of ice cream. Then we started calling him Double Dip.

I guess ice cream made him strong, too, because when he was a young man working in the cotton warehouse he could back up to a bale of cotton with a cotton hook in each hand, bend his knees just a little, sink each hook in the bale behind him with a good solid whack, then stand up, lifting the five-hundred-pound bale about a foot off the floor, and carry it across the warehouse to where it was to be stored. After watching him do this, some of his friends began to call him Da Man, while others called him Double Dip. So his name just naturally worked itself into being Double Dip Da Man, and that's the only name he goes by now. Not only is it that way on the record at Parchman, it's that way on his Social Security card, too.

He married Ammonia, our cook, or rather they were voodooed together, and that's even stronger than being just married, because a divorce can unmarry you but it can't unvoodoo you. You have to find somebody with special powers who is willing to expend some of those powers to take the voodoo off, and there aren't many of those people around these days.

Anyway, Double Dip was there at the back door, and I called to him to come on in. He came into the kitchen with his hand stuck out to me, holding a small scrap of paper, saying as he got closer, "Mist' Jim, can you dial dis hyar number on yo phone?"

The telephone people had just given us folks in Mississippi the dial system, and Double Dip figured that little black horn could reach just about anybody. I looked at the number and saw that it wasn't local and asked him, "Double Dip, where *is* this number?"

"Dat's Lightnin's number over 'bout Bug Scrabble. He da one what married mah baby sister. Our oldest sister, what 'at man married an' tuk off up dere to Detroit, jus' up an' died Friday, an' he won't brang her back hyar fo' buryin', so some uv us chilluns gonna go up dere to the funeral. Lightnin', he s'posed to come by hyar an' pick me up, den we's gonna go on up thru Holly Springs an' git mah middle sister an' her oldes' boy. An Ah wants to see 'bout what time he's comin' thru hyar a'ter us."

Lightning had lived here on the place with us, too, till Minnie May, Double Dip's youngest sister, moved over close to Bug Scrabble, and he just had to leave here and follow her. Bug Scrabble is about twenty-five miles from here. Most of the old folks still call it Bug Scrabble, but the young ones don't, especially the ones who live there. They changed the name to New Harmony. I guess they figured that a town named New Harmony would last longer than one named Old Harmony, and that's what the older folks finally agreed to name it, too—that is, if the young ones just had to change it from Bug Scrabble.

I told Double Dip that I was sorry about his sister and picked up the phone and started putting numbers together so that Lightning's phone would ring over about Bug Scrabble. After I got Double Dip and Lightning connected, I sat down to finish my cup of coffee. From Double Dip's end of the conversation I gathered that Lightning would be here early Tuesday morning. Double Dip hung up the phone and told me what I already knew from what I had just heard. And he went on, " 'At man gonna bury her up dere, an' us chilluns wants to go up dere to see her. We's gonna run up dere Tuesday, an' we'll be back hyar the next day."

I looked at Double Dip and realized that he really believed that. The farthest he had ever been from home, here in Lafayette County, Mississippi, was the state penitentiary, and it had taken him seven years and a lot of promises to be good to get back home from there.

I said, "Double Dip, you can't even get there in a car in the time you say you and Lightning are going to get all the way up there and then back here, too."

Double Dip said, "Aw naw suh, ain't nuthin' 'at fur. Detroit, hit jus' up dere on the udder side uv Memphis."

I told him, "Double Dip, you can go, and I'll help you, but you just can't get there that quick, let alone there and back here the next day. And besides that, I know Lightning, and he even gets lost between here and Bug Scrabble, and that's just twenty-five miles. How in the world are you going to find your way to Detroit and all the way back home, too?"

Double Dip and Lightning had already figured that out.

He said, "We's gotta nephew what can read one uv them maps, an' he gonna go wid us."

I said, "All right, we might not see you again, but let's see about getting you ready. Is Ammonia going with you, too?"

Double Dip said, "Naw suh, she ain't goin'. She done been up dere onct, an' she say she ain't never gonna go back no mo'."

I thought: Thank goodness. The house just about falls apart when Ammonia isn't here.

Double Dip's excitement over his first trip north of Memphis partly compensated for his sorrow over the loss of his sister. We spent the rest of the afternoon and all day Monday getting him ready to meet Lightning on our town square Tuesday morning at six o'clock, the time Lightning said he would be there. Double Dip made at least a dozen trips from their house just down the hill to our house, where Ammonia was working that Monday, to talk about the trip and tell her how to feed his dogs and cows while he was gone.

I overheard one of their conversations about where Detroit is, and Ammonia got exasperated because she couldn't get through to Double Dip just how far Detroit is from here. "Double Dip, you come on out hyar on da front porch an' let me show you sompin what you don't know." Double Dip followed her through the hall and out onto the porch. Ammonia pointed northwest toward the ridge line about five miles away and said, "Double Dip, see 'at line uv trees over yonder? Well, when you's in Detroit, you look way over yonder thataway, an' there's Canada."

Double Dip looked for a minute to where Ammonia was still pointing and finally said, "Hump, ain't nuthin 'at fur 'way from where I'se stanin' rat now." Ammonia slammed her arm down by her side and stomped back down the hall to the kitchen muttering, "You jus' can't tell 'im nuthin.'"

We finally got Double Dip all together, and I took him to meet Lightning at six o'clock Tuesday morning. Lightning was the only one in the car when he stopped to get Double Dip, and I asked him where their nephew was "what can read them maps." They said he was their sister's boy up in Holly Springs and that they would get him when they picked her up. I told them I didn't think even the two of them could get lost between here and Holly Springs, since it is just thirty miles and only one road with no turnoffs.

They left and I settled down for the next few days, wondering just how they would take to Detroit and how Detroit would take to them. The rest of us around the farm took turns doing Double Dip's chores, waiting for him to get back and tell us all about his trip. Double Dip didn't think he would be gone but one night. He expected to be home by Thursday at the latest, but I didn't start looking for him till late Friday.

Saturday morning Ammonia said that Double Dip hadn't come in during the night, but she didn't seem to be at all worried yet. He didn't come in Saturday, and I didn't see him Sunday, either; but Monday morning there he was just as always. He seemed to know every time I planned to go anywhere, because he would leave about five minutes ahead of me, so I would pick him up and give him a ride down the road a piece.

This Monday morning was no different. There he was, strolling down our road that leads to the main road about a half a mile away, in that slow ambling gait of his that never really gets him anyplace but doesn't tire him out walking, either. He was smoking an old black pipe that he always had whether it was burning or not and gazing around at the trees. He acted this morning like he did all other mornings—surprised to see me pull up beside him but knowing all along that I was about to leave the house and that I would stop and give him a ride as far as I was going, or as far as he was going, and it didn't really matter which one came first, because usually he didn't care where I was going, he would go there too, just to see what I was doing.

I said, "Morning, Double Dip. When did you get home?" He got in the car and slammed the door hard enough to rock the whole thing, me included. He shut car doors like he used to slam the doors of an old Model T Ford to make the latch catch. I flinched every time he did it, because I just knew that one time he would break the door, glass and all. He answered, "Yestiddy, Mista' Jim, yassuh, we come in yestiddy." He looked out the right-hand window at the pasture as we drove down to the main road. "We woulda got in Friday night, but when we got back to Holly Springs 'bout ten o'clock Friday night to let mah sister an' her boy out . . ." I broke in and said, "That's the one who read the maps for you, wasn't it?" "Yassuh, 'at da one. Well, we foun' out 'at 'at man what she married had done been in a car wreck an' dey had done sont 'im up to Memphis to da doctor. So we loads back up, an' tuk mah sister an' her boy to Memphis to da hoispi'l where her man wuz at. We got dere 'bout midnight an' let her out at da big hoispi'l up dere, an' she sayed she wuz gonna stay, an' fur us to go on back home 'thout her. Well, suh, mah nephew—'at one what can read 'em maps—'sides he wuz gonna stay in Memphis, too. An 'at's when we got all turnt 'round an' messed up, 'cause we hadn't been payin' no min' to where we done been, or where at we wuz agoin'."

80

Double Dip turned around and looked at me and said, "You know, Mist' Jim, 'at Memphis, 'at 'bout de bigges' town ever I did see in all mah whole life. We driv 'round 'at place from midnight Friday night till 'bout midnight Saddy an' never could fin' no way outen it. 'Bout den I tol' Lightnin' dat ifen he'd jus' pull up an' stop da car, I'd fin' us a way outen hit an' back home."

Double Dip shook his head and went on, "I hadn't no sooner 'en got outen da car good an' walked 'round in one uv them wide roads wid all them lights lit up, fo one uv them policeman's car driv up wid 'at red light cuttin' on an' off." Double Dip looked at me sort of big-eyed and said, " 'At big fella got outen 'at car an' come right up to where I wuz stanin' at, an' ast me what wuz Ah doin' out in da middle uv 'at road. I tol' 'im Ah wuz tryin' to fin' somebody what could tell us how to git back to Mist' Jim's place."

And Double Dip said that the policeman said, "Just who in the hell is this Mist' Jim?"

And Double Dip said he said, " 'At's where Ah stays at." And the policeman asked, "And just where in the hell is that?"

Double Dip said that after he looked up and found the North Star he pointed south and said, "Down yonder." The policeman walked behind the car and looked at the license plate, and after reading the state and county names said, "You want to get back where this car came from, don't you?"

Double Dip said, "Naw suh, 'at car, hit belong to Lightnin' dere, an' he stay over 'bout Bug Scrabble."

The policeman asked, "Where did you say he stays?"

Double Dip said, "Over 'bout Bug Scrabble, you knows where 'at is. 'Bout twenty-five miles from Mist' Jim's place."

The policeman said, "No, I don't know where Bug

Scrabble is. I don't even know what it is." It finally came out somewhere in the conversation that it was in Lafayette County down in Mississippi and that they had been driving around trying to find their way out of Memphis and back home since the night before.

The policeman must have looked at Double Dip like he just couldn't believe this was happening to him, but he didn't know Double Dip and Lightning. He rubbed his chin and told Double Dip to get back in the car and he would lead them out of town and put them back on the road to Mississippi and home. Double Dip said they followed that car with the red light cutting on and off and the siren going all the way out of town to the city limits where the patrol car pulled off on the shoulder of the road and the policeman waved them on and pointed south, telling them to go that way.

Double Dip said he waved at them as they passed, and I'll bet the policeman said to himself, "Please don't come back. The Memphis traffic can't stand too much of this." Double Dip said it wasn't long before they got to Holly Springs after that, and since it was just thirty miles from there to home he wasn't worried about getting lost any more before he got back to Lafayette County.

I had already stopped at the main road just to listen to Double Dip's tale, so I asked, "Double Dip, how did you like it up there in Detroit?"

His eyes got big and he shook his head and said, "Naw suh, Mist' Jim, does you know what? We wuz jus' a settin' dere in 'at 'partment house Thursday mornin' an' a fella come a runnin' in an' sayed dey had done jus' shot a fella down da street fo' twenty dollars, jus' twenty dollars. Livin' up dere is jus' lak rabbits runnin' in front uv da dawgs. Evertime you

82

sticks yo haid up, somebody shoots at you. Naw suh, not me, I'se stayin' rat chere."

I asked Double Dip if he wanted to go back up there, even if it was for just a short visit, and he answered, "Naw suh." Then he looked around at me about half grinning and said, "I done been."

# Aunt Tee
# and Her Two Monuments

OXFORD IS BUILT ON A SQUARE with the court-house in the middle. The founders of the county determined the boundary lines according to the distance a man could travel by horseback or wagon from his farm to the courthouse—leaving at daylight, tending to his business, and returning home before dark.

My family came to Oxford long before the turn of the century. Grandfather was the first one. He had two sons— "Big Dad," who was really my grandfather, and Uncle John—and one daughter, Auntie. We called her Aunt Tee. Big Dad was the oldest; then came Aunt Tee, just a little younger; and last, Uncle John. And there was Uncle Ned, too. He had been born a slave on the same day as Grand-father, and they had belonged to each other ever since.

Big Dad, Uncle John, and Aunt Tee all inherited quick tempers from Grandfather, and Aunt Tee got more than her share. She caused a good many fights, and she was the reason Big Dad was shot in the back and mouth over in Pontotoc one time. Big Dad always said that if Aunt Tee had been a man somebody would have killed her before she was twenty-one.

As far as she was concerned, her family could do no wrong. She always looked after and took up for all her children, as she called her child, grandchildren, nephews, nieces, grand-nephews, and grandnieces.

Aunt Tee wasn't very big in stature, but she was a giant in character and personality; and Nannie, my Falkner grand-mother, was the same way. Aunt Tee and Nannie just had to be good friends, because if they hadn't been, all of Oxford and Lafayette County wouldn't have been big enough for both of them. Aunt Tee's husband, Dr. Porter Wilkins, died shortly after they were married and about the same time that Grandfather's wife died, so Aunt Tee, along with her small daughter, Sallie, moved back into the big house with Grand-father to look after him and run his house and everything and everybody else that came close to her. After that, Grand-father stayed around his bank and law office more than was necessary or than he was wanted, most of the time just to keep out of Aunt Tee's way.

In the late 1800s and early 1900s Southern counties erected a statue of a Confederate soldier on the town square in memory of the men who had served the Lost Cause. Oxford was no exception, but it has two monuments instead of the usual one. Grandfather told me about Aunt Tee's two Con-federate statues one summer night while we were sitting on the front porch after supper waiting for the house to cool off so we could go to bed. He was in his rocking chair and Uncle Ned was dozing in the chair that Grandfather kept behind his just for Uncle Ned. I was sitting on the top step leaning against one of the white square porch columns, where I could watch him and still see out through the old cedar grove that was our front yard.

Aunt Tee and Nannie ran the chapter of the United

85

Daughters of the Confederacy in our town. They ran it to their complete satisfaction, even when the other ladies in the club opposed them. Aunt Tee and Nannie decided that since other towns had honored their Southern soldiers with a statue Oxford should, too. They and the other UDC ladies raised the money for the statue, and Grandfather, who was president and owner of the bank and a lawyer, put in a large share of it. So they ordered the statue. Weeks went by and the statue didn't come. Aunt Tee and Nannie had other things going to keep them and everybody else busy, and the matter of the statue sort of slipped into the background.

Once in a while Grandfather would get a little homesick for our folks over in Haywood County, North Carolina, and he would take some of the family with him for a few weeks' visit. About this time Aunt Tee and Nannie went with him, and it just happened that the statue arrived while they were gone. The rest of the ladies in Aunt Tee's and Nannie's United Daughters of the Confederacy chapter saw a chance to cement relations between Oxford and the University of Mississippi, located a mile west of the town square. They saw the chance, too, to get back at Aunt Tee and Nannie for running their business, and besides, this was what they had wanted to do with the statue in the first place. So they gave it to the university and had it erected on the campus before Aunt Tee and Nannie got back from North Carolina.

Grandfather was telling me all about it that night, and it was funny to him then, but not when it actually happened. He said that they had been home from North Carolina a few days before Aunt Tee found out that her statue had come and that the ladies had already had it erected on the university campus. He said that Aunt Tee and Nannie were out riding in the buggy with Chess driving the two black matched stallions.

(Chess was Grandfather's driver; that is, he was Grandfather's driver only when Aunt Tee decided that she didn't need him.) Then Aunt Tee saw the monument. Her first thought was that somebody had slipped behind her back and had been first to put up a Confederate statue in her area. Then it dawned on her that it was her statue, and that really set her off.

Grandfather said he could have heard her bellow all the way to town if he had just had his office window open. He wasn't long in hearing her, sure enough. Uncle Ned was sitting on a little wooden bench that Grandfather kept for him just outside the bank door, and he was the first to see the two black stallions burst onto the square in a full gallop, pulling that bouncing buggy full of Aunt Tee and Nannie and leaving a cloud of boiling dust behind. Chess was about half standing up, hanging onto the lines trying to keep the stallions from running right on through and out the other side of the town square, and Aunt Tee was about half standing up, too, poking Chess in the back with her parasol and yelling for him to go faster.

Uncle Ned hustled through the front door of the bank and on past the tellers' windows to the back where Grandfather had his office to warn him that Aunt Tee was coming; then he went out the back door to find something to do to keep himself out of Aunt Tee's way when she hit the bank like she always did when she was acting like that. The tellers and clerks couldn't get out when she came in hunting Grandfather, but they always managed to busy themselves as far from Aunt Tee's path as they could, especially when she was on the warpath about something.

Grandfather said that Aunt Tee came in that day like a whirlwind, tapping the floor with the end of her folded-up parasol every step she took right up to his desk. She slammed the parasol on Grandfather's desk and demanded, "Pappy, who in the hell gave my statue to those people out there?"

Grandfather didn't answer right off; he just sat there. He leaned around the corner of his desk and let fly a stream of tobacco juice at the spittoon, then looked up at Aunt Tee, still standing there fuming. He demanded back, "How in the hell could I know anything like that without you already knowing it first?"

Aunt Tee whirled around and stomped and tapped her way out the door muttering, "I damn sure will find out who in the hell did what, and somebody will either move that one to town or get me another one just like it."

Hearing Aunt Tee leave, Uncle Ned poked his head around Grandfather's office door and asked, "Marse Will, is we gonna go to da house fo' dinna now dat Missy done got herself all lathered up?" Grandfather thought a minute and said, "No, you'd better step next door to Buck's store and fetch us some cheese and crackers. We'll let her calm down some, then go home about supper time."

But Aunt Tee didn't calm down; in fact, she had the whole house and the biggest part of the neighborhood treed by he time Grandfather and Uncle Ned got there, even though they did wait longer than usual to go home. Uncle Ned saw the mood she was in just as soon as he and Grandfather got in sight of her; so he made his way to the kitchen before Aunt Tee could unload any of her wrath on him, but Grandfather caught it all.

Aunt Tee was really mad about that statue she and Nannie had planned to have erected on the courthouse lawn. The other ladies had given it away and already had it up before she knew anything about it, and she and Nannie wouldn't even get any credit for it from those people out there, as she called the folks who were connected with the school. Supper that night was quieter than usual, with the silence broken only by Aunt Tee's muttering, "It's my statue and they gave it to those people out there, and I'm going to get it back or have another one just like that one."

Grandfather said the only thing he could do at a time like that was to keep his mouth shut, because if he said anything at all, he knew it would be wrong; so he finished his supper, folded his napkin in a triangle as he always did, and said, "Thank you for my supper," as he always did, and went to his rocking chair on the front porch. He had just settled back with his feet propped up on the banister rail and a fresh plug of tobacco in the side of his mouth to watch the town go to sleep when Aunt Tee came out the front door, still stomping and tapping. Grandfather looked at Aunt Tee, then at the parasol, then back at Aunt Tee, and said, "Missy, wherever you are going, it's first dark now and you won't need that parasol to keep the sun off."

Aunt Tee stopped halfway down the steps and stopped stomping, but she didn't stop tapping. "It doesn't look like you are going to do a damn thing about my statue," she said, "so I am. I'll either get that one back or they will get me another one just like it. I already had a place picked out for it on the south side of the courthouse yard with it facing down South Street towards this house, and besides that I don't use this parasol just to keep the sun off."

Grandfather said to himself, "I don't doubt that at all," as he watched Aunt Tee parasol-tap down the wooden sidewalk in the direction of Nannie's house; and he said that he hoped, too, that nobody, especially one of those people from out there, would be unfortunate enough to be caught in her path that night. The next morning at breakfast Grandfather thought things might have calmed down a bit, but Aunt Tee's eyes were still flashing and she was still saying, "It's mine and I'm going to have it, or one just like it."

About that time Grandfather had had enough, and he knew it wouldn't get any better, so he slammed his hand and napkin down on the table so hard that it made the dishes and silverware jump and clatter and told Aunt Tee that if she would just shut up about it he would buy her a damn statue and she could set it any damn place she damn well pleased.

Aunt Tee took Grandfather at his word. She was in the bank that morning before he had a chance to get settled good. "Where is the money for my statue?" Grandfather looked up at that and said, "By God, now you are going to own two of them. Go ahead and order it. I'll pay for it when it comes."

Aunt Tee did order the statue that day, and she didn't let its arrival slip up on her this time. She kept in touch with the maker and the railroad so that nobody could put anything over on her again. The station agent at the depot said that if that monument didn't come soon he would either quit or ask for a transfer. Aunt Tee acted like it was all his fault each day when the train came in and her statue wasn't on it.

Finally the statue did come in one morning, and the railroad man had no sooner unloaded it from the boxcar into the freight wagon than Aunt Tee and Nannie appeared with all their ladies—whether they liked it or not, and most of them didn't—to stand around paying tribute to the symbol of the memory of the boys in gray from our county who had given their all for the cause. The trip to the town square was solely directed by Nannie and Aunt Tee, and the wagon carrying the statue was escorted by their ladies, again whether they wanted to or not, because they were directed by Aunt Tee, too, as was the driver of the wagon.

The concrete foundation, already poured at Aunt Tee's direction on the south lawn of the courthouse, sat just waiting for the monument. When the procession reached the court-house yard, most of the businessmen along the route and on the square, the courthouse people, and nearly everybody else in sight gathered around, not to direct—because they knew that Aunt Tee would do that—but to help get the statue upright on its foundation.

When it was up and in place, Aunt Tee backed off and stood with her left hand on her hip and her right hand resting on her parasol looking up at the life-size Confederate soldier standing on top of the twenty-foot pedestal looking down South Street towards Grandfather's house, one knee slightly bent in an easy standing position, with the rifle butt between his feet and both hands resting on the barrel.

He stood there atop the marble pedestal with the engraving on the base:

IN MEMORY OF
THE PATRIOTISM OF THE
CONFEDERATE SOLDIERS
OF LAFAYETTE COUNTY
MISSISSIPPI

THEY GAVE THEIR LIVES
IN A JUST AND HOLY CAUSE

Grandfather said they should have a dedication ceremony and somebody had to make a speech. He said he couldn't let Aunt Tee be the whole show, because she was hard enough to get along with just being most of it, so he told Nannie that she would have to do it. That suited Nannie just fine because she figured she was still fighting the Big War anyway and this would give her the opportunity to fire another shot for her cause. They picked a Saturday afternoon in August after laying-by time, so all the folks from out in the county would be in town for the big event.

Aunt Tee and Nannie saw to the building of a wooden platform big enough for a speaker's stand and the local band, and Grandfather saw to it that it was big enough for the town fathers, too. After all, it was their land that the statue would stand on forever, and Grandfather thought that Aunt Tee and Nannie should show them some small bit of acknowledgment, whether they wanted to or not.

The big day came. The monument was covered with Confederate flags that would fall away at just the right time when Uncle Ned pulled the string at Nannie's signal, revealing the soldier staring south over the crowd down South Street towards Grandfather's house. The platform below the statue was gaily decorated, and the band was playing "The Yellow Rose of Texas" and other Southern songs. The square was packed with grown-ups and children and dogs and horses and mules. The grown-ups were listening to the band and talking about their crops, the children were chasing each other, the dogs were fighting, and the horses and mules were just standing in the shade switching flies. At just the right time the band struck up "Dixie." The men cheered, and the women cried, and I guess some of the men had tears, too, because some of them were old enough to remember it all.

When the band stopped, it was Nannie's time. She stepped across the platform to the speaker's stand and gave the signal to Uncle Ned, who was holding the string attached to the flags that were covering the statue. He gave a good healthy jerk and the flags drifted down and away from the confederate soldier and settled at the base of the monument.

Nannie looked up at the statue, then back at the crowd.

Her eyes were flashing black. She pointed upwards at the soldier. She was still looking at the crowd, and her eyes were still black and flashing. "If I had my way about it, that soldier wouldn't be facing south and his gun wouldn't be at rest."

With that, Nannie whirled and went back to her seat beside Aunt Tee. Aunt Tee reached over and patted Nannie's hand and said, "You are right, Sis Maud, you are so right."

# Grandfather
# Crossing the Creek

G RANDFATHER'S HOUSE is an old two-story house with four white wood columns on the front porch. It sits in a grove of cedar trees back off the little country road that used to be the main road from Oxford to Memphis. This is the same road that General Nathan Bedford Forrest rode down the night he slipped around General A. J. Smith's right flank and made his famous raid on Memphis. Grandfather was with him on that ride and nearly all of his other raids and battles, too, until he was shot in the leg at Franklin trying to protect Hood's retreat. He and Uncle Ned made it back home to this same house with the minié ball still in his knee, and there it stayed as long as he lived, because the doctor said it would do more harm getting it out than just leaving it. Anyway, it gave the Old Colonel something to talk about besides that finger that got shot off down in Mexico during that war. That minié ball in his knee and the lost finger never did stop him from doing anything if he really wanted to do it.

At night after supper in the wintertime Grandfather would sit in his rocking chair in front of the fire staring at the flames as they flickered around the slow-burning logs. His blue-gray eyes were made even grayer by his snow white hair and mustache, but they were still clear and penetrating even after ninety-odd years. Uncle Ned would walk in from the kitchen a short time after he had finished supper. He sat next to the hearth on the stool that Grandfather always kept there for him.

Uncle Ned was born on the same day as Grandfather in a slave cabin down behind the Big House. They had been together every day since then. Even when Grandfather went off to the Big War at the head of his cavalry troop, Uncle Ned went with him as his body servant. Uncle Ned acted like he owned Grandfather rather than Grandfather owning him. Grandfather said that Lincoln had freed the slaves from us, but that nobody had ever freed us from them.

Uncle Ned would settle on his stool by the fire, resting his back against the wall with his arms on his knees and his gnarled old black hands hanging lax nearly to the tops of his shoes. He wouldn't move again except to poke up the fire or put on another log when the flames dwindled down and let a chill creep through his tired old body, and he always had to fix the fire at least once before it suited him. When Uncle Ned got settled again, it was usually the signal for Grandfather to begin his stories about the Big War.

Father's chair was at the other end of the hearth. He would sit there reading the newspaper about half listening to the stories that he had heard many times before while sitting on his fireside bench. Now I pulled the same bench up next to Grandfather's chair. Sometimes I would have to prompt him by saying, "Grandfather, tell me about Brice's Cross Roads where you and Uncle Ned and General Forrest whipped Ole Sturgis so bad," or maybe Father would say to me, "Get him to tell you about how they caught Streight's Raiders over in Georgia."

Grandfather would shift around in his chair until he was comfortable, most of the time with his arms resting on the chair arms and his head a little forward, watching the fire. He always began by saying, "Well, sir, that was when we were up around Ripley" (or wherever the story took place). Uncle Ned would nod his head in affirmation, and Grandfather would launch into the story with the same enthusiasm he had had when he actually experienced the battle. The soldiers became real to him again as he gazed steadily at the fire. His eyes would dilate with the excitement of the coming battle, then narrow to fine points, turning almost black with anger during the fury of the fighting. The flames licking around the logs must have been flashes from the enemy's rifle barrels and the popping of the fire was the sound of exploding shells, because he would get tense all over and his knuckles would turn white from gripping the chair arms as he relived the battle that had happened some sixty years before. About this point in the story Father would put down his paper and listen, even though he had heard it many times, and Uncle Ned would open his eyes and watch Grandfather. Uncle Ned had not only just heard the tale, he had actually been there when it had happened, not because he had to be there or even wanted to be but because he wanted to be near Grandfather. Father had been there, too, once. Grandfather and Uncle Ned and their cavalry were camped close to home here, and they let Father (he was eight years old then) come out and stay with them for a few days.

I could tell when the fight was almost over (Grandfather and Uncle Ned and General Forrest always won) when he began to relax and Uncle Ned's eyes slowly closed and he drifted back to sleep. I think Mother listened, too, because she would come in from the kitchen about this time, where she had been telling Minnie, the cook, what to have for tomorrow, and tell me to get ready to go to bed. That would break the spell for me, but I would go to sleep thinking about Grandfather on his white stallion, Pompus, that his men had stolen from the Yankees on one of their raids and had given to him. He would ride Pompus at the head of his cavalry troop, Uncle Ned trailing along behind in the supply wagon with no real interest in the happenings around him, contented just because Grandfather was nearby.

In the summertime after supper we would sit on the front porch waiting for the house to be cooled by the gentle night breeze that comes across the wide valley and up the hill through the tall old cedar trees that line the brick walk and stand in rows in the front yard. Grandfather had his rocking chair on one side of the front door with Uncle Ned's cane-bottom chair behind him next to the wall. Father's chair was on the other side of the door, and my place was on the top step leaning back against one of the columns that run up past the balcony and support the porch ceiling two stories up. I could sit back and watch Grandfather as he told about the Big War and at the same time listen to the breeze in the cedar trees and the night sounds that are in the country on a warm summer night and imagine that I was with him in all his escapades.

The night it happened was just like many other July nights that we had spent on the porch listening to the sounds of the creatures that come to life after dark, waiting for the house to cool off. Grandfather was gently rocking and Father had put his paper down because it was first dark now and not light enough to read by. I was waiting for Uncle Ned to come around the side of the house from the kitchen and take his customary place behind Grandfather in that cane-bottom chair that was kept there especially for him. We could hear the whippoorwills calling from the peach trees in the edge of the garden and the bull frogs' deep croaking from down by the creek.

Captain, my bird dog, trotted across the yard and up the steps and flopped down beside me just in time to have to move to make way for Uncle Ned. He had finished his supper, too, and had come to take his seat behind Grandfather and doze till bedtime. A few years before, we had moved back to the old family home where Grandfather had spent most of his life except those few years when we had lived in town in the big white house on South Street that he had built so he could be close to his law office and the bank that he had started but had been voted out of because he was hard of hearing. The people doing business with him had to shout to be heard, and they didn't want to broadcast their business. After Aunt Tee and Nannie had caused all that ruckus about the two monuments of Confederate soldiers, he was ready to come back to his country home and live in peace. So we did. Uncle Ned slept on a cot in Grandfather's room just to be there in case Grandfather needed him or he needed Grandfather during the night.

Grandfather seemed more tired than usual that night; he detached himself from us, and two or three times turned around to be sure that Uncle Ned was there. Father waited a while before he leaned over and whispered to me, "Get him to tell you about the raid on Memphis."

I looked at Grandfather and realized for the first time that he was an old man. He was staring out through the trees, and he seemed to be seeing something that I couldn't see. His head was turned slightly to one side, listening for a sound that was strange to the night sounds, and one that I tried to hear but couldn't. I felt a chill between my shoulder blades as I watched him searching and listening. Father felt it, too, because he was watching Grandfather's eyes and trying to follow their stare through the darkness to see what had upset him. Uncle Ned was watching them both, concerned for Grandfather, but feeling as I did that Father knew what was happening but couldn't tell us.

Suddenly Grandfather settled back in his chair and looked around at us as if realizing for the first time that we were there. He turned to see that Uncle Ned was behind him, then smiled at me and said, "Well, son, which one would you like to hear tonight?"

"The one I like best is the raid on Memphis."

He said, "Well, sir, I do, too. That was back in July and August of sixty-four when old Sherman was raising hell over in Georgia, and they sent Smith down from Memphis to keep us busy, so we couldn't jump on Sherman's supply line and make him dry up and die right in front of Joe Johnston there at Atlanta.

"We were over close to Okolona waiting for Smith to commit himself. When he did turn south at Holly Springs and head for Oxford, we aimed for Oxford, too. He got here just a few hours before we did, but when we came over River's Hill out there east of town, he hightailed it back across Harrikin Creek, and there he sat with twenty thousand men and us with just fifty-five hundred. Well, sir, we just sat there and shot at each other for ten days knowing that we couldn't hold them back long, but knowing, too, that old Bedford would come up with something. He always did.

"The night General Forrest pulled that raid, me and Ned had run out here to see how your grandmother and everybody were getting along with all the shooting and troops moving around this close to the house and to get a good supper for a change. I was resting in this same chair in this same spot just about first dark that night when I heard a cavalry troop moving down that road right there." He was pointing at the old road that ran in front of the house and leaning forward trying to see, getting caught up in the excitement now and living again that night in 1864. He stopped telling it as a story then and was actually living in it. He reached back and touched Uncle Ned and said, "Ned, listen, I can hear horses coming. Can you tell who they are?" His face was more flushed than usual this time, and his eyes had a wild excited look as he stared up the road towards town where General Forrest had come from that night over a half a century earlier.

Uncle Ned was almost standing up, looking first at Grandfather, then out in the trees, trying to see what he was seeing. Father had dropped the paper and was leaning forward looking at Grandfather, too, trying to follow his searching stare to find out what was taking place beyond the dark shadows along the old road. The whippoorwills stopped calling to one another, and the bullfrogs quit their croaking. All the night life was quiet. A ghostly silence and calm settled around us. I had my hand on Captain's head trying to hold on to something, but he eased down the steps with his tail drooping. When he got around the corner of the house, he sat down and pointed his nose to the sky. His low mournful howl broke the quiet and sent shivers through all of us except Grandfather, and made me, a twelve-year-old boy, want to crawl up in Father's lap to get away from whatever was happening out there in our front yard.

The moon was up now, making pools of light underneath the cedar trees. I could imagine anything and everything in the

100

soft moonlight, and I think Father and Uncle Ned could, too. I know Grandfather saw something. I think I really did hear horses trotting down the road that night with the saddle leather creaking under the weight of the Confederate cavalry troopers and the sabre chain's soft metallic tinkle.

Grandfather wasn't saying anything now, just listening. He had his head turned slightly to one side, trying to hear better. Suddenly he turned to Uncle Ned and said, "Ned, did you hear the sergeant tell us that General Forrest said to get ready, that we had to ride tonight, and he would wait for us across the creek? Hurry now, go get your bay mare and saddle Pompus while I get dressed. The General won't wait long. Make haste, now!"

Father and Uncle Ned were on their feet standing by Grandfather. I could tell by the worried expression on both their faces that something was happening. Uncle Ned took Grandfather by the arm and said, "Yassuh, Marse Bill, Ah'll git them hosses ready, but fust let's git yo fightin' suit on."

Father nodded at Uncle Ned and each took one of Grandfather's arms and gently raised him from the rocking chair. I held one of the double screen doors open while they guided him slowly into the house and turned right to his bedroom. It seemed to be an effort for Grandfather to get to the bed, even with Father and Uncle Ned helping him at each elbow. He lay down there on the bed with his snow white hair softly splayed on the pillow and his eyes not so fierce now, gazing around the ceiling, and his face paling some in the flickering lamplight. Still living that night in the past, he said, "Ned, get my suit and the flag, then bring the horses up. The General is waiting for us across the creek."

Uncle Ned glanced up at Father with a puzzled look in his

old faded brown eyes from where he was kneeling beside Grandfather's bed. Father nodded, then turned to me and said, "Go find your mother and ask her to call Dr. Clifford and tell him that we need him now."

When I told her what Father had said, I think she already knew there was no real need, but she went to the wall phone and turned the crank for Central anyway, as I tiptoed back into Grandfather's room and stood next to the bed beside Father, who was sitting at the foot watching Uncle Ned button the Confederate colonel's tunic on Grandfather. When he finished, he laid the battle flag on the bed next to Grandfather's hand.

Grandfather's eyes were still drifting from one familiar object to another until they came to rest on me. He held out his hand to me and said, "Come here, Johnny."

Father said in a whisper, "Go to him. He thinks you are me."

Grandfather held my hand and said to Uncle Ned, "We'll have to let him camp with us the next time we are close to home."

His hand was cool and weak and I was scared, because I knew by then that he was more than just sick or tired. He closed his eyes as if he were resting before going to meet the General. Father put his hand on my shoulder and gently pulled me back to stand beside him. Uncle Ned was on his knees by the bed holding Grandfather's hand, watching his face, and listening to his shallow breathing.

Grandfather stirred a little and opened his eyes. As they opened they focused on me. He smiled faintly, then shifted them to Father, who was standing over him now holding his other hand; then they moved to Uncle Ned and he said to him, barely loud enough for us to hear, "Across the creek."

His eyes closed and he relaxed. Uncle Ned put his ear to Grandfather's chest; he listened a minute, then pushed his head closer, trying to hear the faintest sound of a heartbeat; then he raised up and looked at Father with tears running down his old wrinkled brown cheeks and in a quivering voice said, "Marse Johnny, he didn't wait fo' me."

Father put his arm around Uncle Ned's shoulders and said, "Uncle Ned, he and the General can't get along without you. They are both waiting for you across the creek."

MIDDLEBURY COLLEGE